REACHING

FOR

FIREFLIES

Decisions That Extended My Grasp

ED TAR

A Memoir

eta

ETA Publishing

California

Copyright © 2021

ISBN: 978-1-7377699-0-3 (Paperback)
ISBN: 978-1-7377699-1-0 (eBook)
Library of Congress Control Number: 2021917465

Library of Congress
US Programs, Law and Literature Division
Cataloging in Publication Program
101 Independence Avenue, S.E.
Washington, DC 20540-4283

Events in this book are memories from the author's perspective.
Book Design: Acapella Cover Design. Jennifer Givner
All Photos: Personal
Printed by Book Baby, Inc., in the United States of America.
First printing edition 2021

Publisher:
ETA Publishing
230 Venice Way
Venice, CA 90291
www.edtarauthor.com

PRAISE

"Bravo! Reaching for Fireflies is an engaging account of one man's life experiences, rich in historical detail from the pen of a gifted story teller. Even more, it is an invaluable blueprint for anyone blessed with the courage, passion and conviction to chart his or her own course in Life. A must read!"

"Incredibly well written. I started reading and I could not stop. I can feel the struggle. It's amazing."

— *Michael Stein, Former UCLA Law Professor*

"You're an accomplished writer and story teller. The story telling is on a high level and was most engaging. I kept reading as it pulled me along. The descriptions are well done and the action moved nicely. Congratulations."

— *Paul Edward Gainor author of Human's and Other Animals*

"This book is an easy and wonderful read. It brings back our own memories of how we grew up and relates to the excitement, struggles and fun the author eloquently describes. No matter your background or age, you will dream about your own life and how you dealt with similar issues."

— *Robert King, Financial Advisor, MGO International*

"It held my attention and was an interesting read. Great job on it!"

— *Matt Miller, former CEO, Newmar Corporation*

"I found your book well written and the stories of your experiences kept my interest. I'm sure others will feel the same way."

— *John D..Hofbauser, M.D.*

"In *Reaching For Fireflies*, author Ed Tar reveals the power of the human spirit to overcome negative influences in the mystery and light of possibility."

— *Paul Crouch, Jr. Chairman,Cinemills Corp.*
— *Brenda Crouch, Author of Fight Forward*

"Loved it. Great stories and great story telling. I wanted more. Route 66 must have been great to drive."

— *Donald Trepany, DC*

"I just loved your book. You are spot on! You are a wonderful story teller. It was if I was in your house experiencing everything you were experiencing. Wishing you success."

— *Joe Torrenueva, Entrepreneur*

"I really enjoyed it. It was so good, I just got caught up in the story and wanted more."

— *Justin White, Managing Director, Centennial Advisors*

"What you sent me was great!"

— *Gerry Byrne, Vice Chairman, Penske Media Corporation*

To Pat, who has always been my inspiration with her unending love, creative spirit, warm heart, curiosity, and "can do" attitude.

ACKNOWLEDGMENTS

When doubts entered my mind about writing this book, I was fortunate to discover a group of talented writers and authors who, in one sense, were the foundation from which I gained the confidence to continue to move forward.

It was in Author Suzanne Sherman's wonderful memoir and writing classes that I met these glimmering fireflies: Paula Fayerman, Paula Girolo, Kathleen Gallagher, Dan Muntz, Lyle Norton, Alice Perlman and Judy Watten. They are all accomplished writers, who generously offered me advice, encouragement and critical critiques of my work. They picked me up when the right words just wouldn't come out on the paper and they kept me going as I sought to extend my grasp for stories that would touch the reader.

I had the opportunity to experience and witness how they skillfully and professionally crafted their own work, and am forever grateful to them for sharing their talent, their enthusiasm and their knowledge. Thank you all.

CHAPTER 1

I stood there stunned as my mother and brother carefully lowered my father's violently shaking body onto the living room floor. As an eight-year-old, I had never seen that happen before, and the frightening image left an indelible mark on my mind that was never to go away.

Up until that point, the activity at home that warm summer afternoon had been nothing unusual; it was busy. My mother was setting the dining room table for an early Sunday dinner. She spread out the tablecloth, running her hands over it to smooth the wrinkles and carefully adjusted it so the cloth hung evenly on all sides. Then she reached for the key on top of the nearby china cabinet to unlock it and retrieve a couple of special plates. With a house full of kids, the key was out of sight and the cabinet was kept locked so we wouldn't get into it on a whim and potentially damage anything—most regular dishes were in the kitchen cabinets. I heard the light clinking of dishes as the table was being set; my sister Rosemary was helping, as she usually did.

Meanwhile, my older brother Frank and sister Irene were back and forth through the house. I was in the living room playing with the latest promotional rings that came as prizes inside the Cheerios box. I had an entire collection, including one from the box with the Lone Ranger's picture. My father was going through his Sunday ritual. He never went to church and was upstairs sleeping in late—he usually stirred and awoke around 1 p.m. My mother was always concerned that we kids would make too much noise and wake him, so she kept telling us to keep quiet or go outside. We had felt his anger a couple of times before when we had happened to wake him. He would curse and complain about not being able to "sleep in at least one day a week" and could make everyone feel uneasy for the remainder of the day.

Soon, we heard his bath water running. The shower never worked as the old pipes and showerhead had to be completely replaced and we didn't have any money to do that. In a short while, he was on the stairs, gripping the handrail for support as he gingerly walked down. His legs hurt constantly due to his failing veins and poor circulation, and standing for eight hours a day all week at the Ford factory didn't help that situation.

Clean-shaven and smelling of lilac aftershave, he wore his standard Sunday outfit: a white tank top undershirt, casual dark pants, and those ever-present white socks and black shoes. Occasionally, he seemed happy with a slight smile, but not today. Today, he seemed unsettled. He walked across the living room, leaning slightly forward like he might fall over at any moment. At only about five foot nine, his leaning body made him look even shorter. He said, "Why the hell can't you all be quiet so I can get some sleep?"

My mother, always sensitive to his moods, attempted to ignore what he said as she greeted him. "Lou (his name was Louis), how are you feeling today? Dinner will be ready shortly."

He repeated, "Why can't those kids be quiet once in a while?"

I tried to stay out of his way and said nothing.

He took a quick walk into the kitchen, then back to the

living room where he picked up the newspaper and sat down in his favorite stuffed corner chair, putting his legs up on the footstool in front of it. He opened the paper and hid behind its wide double pages, looking at the horse racing results. All seemed normal, and we knew the drill. With his pencil, he wrote the race results on the paper's margins (I saw the pencil scribbles once and had no idea what they meant). He played the horses regularly, and the Sunday paper contained Saturday's race results. Once in a while, he would actually win, and those few extra dollars were appreciated: most weeks, he didn't bring home enough money to pay the bills and keep the refrigerator stocked. He wasn't facing the reality and held on to the dream that one day he would "hit it big," as I heard him say to my mother, who normally replied, "Yeah, yeah, big shot; I've heard all that before. I don't care about hitting it big, I just want you to bring home a full paycheck—I can't make it on the twelve dollars you bring home every week." That usually touched his hot button and started an argument.

We could smell dinner cooking in the kitchen, when all of a sudden, my mother screamed, "Your father's having a seizure!" My brother and sister seemed startled; I wasn't sure what was going on. We looked up. He didn't appear any different, but behind the newspaper, he was. How my mother knew about his seizures was beyond me, but she had a sixth sense about his behavior and knew—even before he did, sometimes—what was happening. She ran into the living room as his hands fell, crumpling the newspaper. He gave out a loud cry and a moan, and his entire body started to tremble and stiffen.

She grabbed him and yelled to my brother, "Frank, hurry! Help me get him down onto the floor." At the same time, she told my sisters, "Quick, bring me a spoon." There was no panic on her part, just fast action to take care of something she'd seen and dealt with before.

They laid him on the living room carpet as the shaking

and screaking intensified. He was foaming at the mouth. I saw his eyes rolling back, and his body was out of control. My sister handed a spoon to my mother, who steadied his head and placed the handle in his mouth so he wouldn't bite his tongue. She held it there. "Now, get me a towel," she said.

I stood there as the scene was playing out. Down on her knees, my mother looked up at me and said, "Eddie, go outside." I hesitated. She repeated sternly, "Eddie, go outside *now!*"

I took a step toward the living room door, and Frank tried to reassure me, "You'd better go out. Don't worry, he's going to be ok." I stepped out onto the front porch—I'm unsure for how long—but alone and not knowing what was going on, I slowly opened the door and went back in.

My mother looked up and gave me an annoyed glance. She was leaning over my father lying on the floor, talking quietly, and giving directions to my brother and sister: "Ok, I'm going to take the spoon out, he's calming down. Get me another towel to rest his head on."

I looked at my father as his body seemed to be relaxing. My mother was soothingly talking to him: "It's okay, Lou. You had a seizure. Everything is okay." He looked confused, tried to talk and even get up, but she held his head and put a towel under it, saying, "Lou, just stay down. You're fine."

He focused a little and looked directly at me. Our eyes met. I saw a helpless look of panic and fear in his eyes—or was he reflecting what he saw in my eyes?

He mumbled to my mother, "Get the kids out of here."

"They're all right," she answered, wiping his brow. "They were a big help."

A few minutes went by as he rested, then they slowly helped him sit up. Several more minutes passed before they assisted him back into the chair.

Gathering himself, looking self-conscious and embarrassed, he said, "You kids shouldn't see this."

"We're fine," Frank replied, picking up the towels. I couldn't say anything and was still trying to take in all that had just happened. A grand mal seizure is no fun to see, but for an eight-year-old, when it's your father, it can be downright traumatic. I'd heard similar sounds coming from my parents' bedroom before, but the door was always closed and I wasn't allowed near the bedroom, so I wasn't sure what all the scrambling was about.

From that moment on, I always felt a level of anxiety when alone with my father. If it happened, could I handle it? I rehearsed in my mind: lay him down so he doesn't fall, put a spoon or wooden clothespin between his teeth so he doesn't swallow or bite his tongue. Be calm. He will come out of it.

My mother constantly worried about my father driving, especially when he skipped taking the medication that controlled his seizures. I often heard them arguing about it.

He would scream, "I don't need to take those goddamn pills!"

"Yes, you do, or you'll have an attack," she would reply, threatening to report him to the police who might revoke his driver's license. She acted on those threats one time ("for his own good," she said) when he had a minor accident. We felt the ramifications at home as the cussing and arguments intensified.

My father, an only child, was born in 1902 in the small town of Mezőcsát, Hungary—ninety miles northeast of Budapest. With a population of about five thousand people, it was noted for a few mills and a few banks at the time. The main building in town is the *Református Templon*, the Reformed Church, where my father was christened and has his name clearly entered in the church registry that dates back to the eighteenth century. The church in Mezőcsát remains active. It resembles a museum inside with striking, tall, arched. stained-glass windows, fresco-style paintings on the high ceiling, ornate hand-carved chandeliers, and dark wooden doors, columns, and pews that appear to have been hand-polished for decades. It sits next to the school my father attended, and that school is still educating students today.

My grandfather, Karoly Tar, was a former officer in the Royal Hungarian Army and a war hero. His name is engraved, along with those of six others, on a heroes' war monument that sits in front of Mezőcsát City Hall. After he died when my father was six years old, my father and grandmother, Jolan Tar, stayed in Mezőcsát, where he continued to attend school through the fourth grade. Never one to hesitate, my grandmother soon remarried. My father didn't say much about his stepfather, only that he was a banker, and they had servants, something he'd never had before. In 1911, at the age of nine years old, my father came to New York with his mother and stepfather—as tourists, not refugees, to avoid the lengthy processing on Ellis Island. Something happened, and for some reason, his stepfather returned to Hungary. My father stayed in New York with his mother, where they settled down to live. No one knows for sure why or how her second marriage ended, but the assumption is that there was a divorce because in Detroit years later, Jolan married for the third time. Her third husband died just three years after that.

My father never spoke at length about growing up in New York, but I heard him say once, "Everything moved quickly and I had to have street smarts to survive there." He attended public school on the Lower East Side, but not speaking English and being raised alone by his mother, I can only imagine how difficult it must have been to get on in the city.

At age fifteen, he got a job driving and repairing cars at the Mercedes Repair Co. on East 54ᵗʰ Street. I think that's possibly when his love of automobiles began. At nineteen, he received a letter of recommendation from the company president. When he and my grandmother moved to Detroit shortly thereafter, he was proud of that letter and carried it with him to present when applying for a job.

My father finally found his footing in Detroit. He was young and ambitious, and all the important automobile companies were there: Chrysler, General Motors, Ford, Dodge, Packard, Rickenbacker Motors. He worked at Rickenbacker for a short time and had big dreams.

It was the roaring twenties, and he was enjoying it. He frequented the Grande Ballroom on Grand River Avenue near downtown Detroit. It was a famous popular dance hall rumored to be a hangout for the infamous Detroit Purple Gang, and in the twenties, featured many of the top bands in the country. One ad read:

The Grande Ballroom: A most beautiful dance place built with the idea of giving the dancing public a finer, smarter, and cleaner place to dance. Music by the famous dance band The Victors. Admission: Ladies 50 cents. Men 75 cents.

The Grande had a long run, and its final show was on New Year's Eve, 1972.

It was at the Grande that my father met my mother, Rose Schultz. She was a Catholic girl—the third oldest in a family of nine kids—with a strong will and work ethic. Rose was the one in her family whom everyone looked to for advice. She stood tall and straight, appearing rather stern and serious, but this all changed once the music started. She loved to dance, laugh, and have a good time, and she never wanted to leave the dance floor. I was told she and my father had the best times happily dancing together. My mother said once, "Your father was an excellent dancer, and all the girls wanted to dance with the young, good-looking guy from New York, but I got him."

After a whirlwind romance, they were married in St. Francis Catholic Church in Detroit in March 1925. He was two months shy of twenty-three, and she had just turned nineteen. The twenties were indeed roaring for them.

He liked to gamble and take chances, and one of his favorite places to do so was in Toledo, Ohio. My mother didn't want anything to do with gambling, so to entice her to go to Toledo with him, he brought her "sleek, black, sparkling dresses" to wear. Though she didn't like going to Toledo to gamble, she did like the dresses, and to please him, she caved in.

By the time the Depression began, my sister Marge and brother Chuck had already been born. My brother, Frank, and sisters, Irene and Rosemary, were born during the dark Depression days of the early 1930s. Times were tough, especially with five kids, but the Depression hadn't broken our father or reined him in just yet. He was earning enough to buy a small house early in the 30s as well as a Hupmobile—a stylish, luxurious automobile—though it was a gamble to own such a car when they didn't have much money. My mother didn't want the car and quickly told him, "We need the money not a fancy car. Sell it."

I sensed the Depression slowed down my father's dream of making it big in the auto industry, and maybe that's why he gambled.

When I was born, World War II had already begun as Germany rolled through Poland and was beginning to roll across Europe. Meanwhile, the United States was about to get a kick in the face by Japan at Pearl Harbor.

I was too young to understand what was going on at the time, but at home, we were growing our own fruit and vegetables. I had also heard the word 'rationing' and knew we were saving the few tin cans we had.

To help make ends meet, my mother worked for a while rolling cigars at the Webster Cigar Factory in Detroit. Growing up, I heard her mention this a couple of times and thought it was an odd job, as neither she nor my father ever smoked. My mother also worked in a factory during part of the war, and when I heard the term, *Rosie the Riveter*, I thought for the longest time they were talking about her, as her name was Rose. But it was a nickname given to all working women during the war and made famous on a poster with an iconic image of a woman with a red bandanna holding up a strong arm with the caption, "We can do it." The war also brought a serious health crisis for my father that would affect our family from then on. He had his first epileptic seizure during the war years while working eight to ten hours a day testing airplane engines as a lead mechanic at Ford's huge Willow Run plant outside of Detroit. They were building planes for the war effort. He worked in an enclosed area with those loud engines and minimal ear protection—little was required. Doctors said the noise and constant pressure of the heavy plane engines put added pressure on his brain and could have caused brain damage. They added that severe blows to the head could also cause damage, but he said he hadn't hit his head.

He was proud, and I believe from then on, he was insecure, sensitive, and defensive due to his epilepsy.

Doctors told him they may be able to cure his seizures. They wanted to drill a hole in his skull to relieve the pressure on his brain and possibly perform brain surgery.

My father turned to my mother, who was adamant, and without hesitation, said, "They're not going to drill a hole in your head when they can't guarantee a brain operation would be successful to stop those seizures. And they can't even guarantee you would survive such an operation. No! That's not going to happen." It didn't.

CHAPTER 2

E ven through the eyes of a kid, it's safe to say, the kitchen in our house was small. It was unimpressive and had a window over the sink that looked like it had been painted too often without removing the previous layers of paint first. A second window was next to the old gas range that we had to light with a match, and the linoleum in front of the stove and the kitchen sink was wearing thin.

There was a cove with a table—sort of like a Murphy bed—that folded down from the wall, but we kept the table folded up and used that space for a refrigerator. It was one of those small, single-door Hotpoint refrigerators that were popular in the late 40s. Inside, it looked the same as it always did, and the emptiness seemed to make that refrigerator light even brighter, as if to brag, "Look at me!" In most homes, the shelves would probably be full, but not our shelves. We had a refrigerator; never full, but I had hopes it might be one day.

That refrigerator was a big leap up from the small Depression-era icebox we used to have. The icebox wasn't used much during the winter, as we placed the food that needed to remain cold—meat, butter, and milk—on the ledge between the window and its screen. They stayed cold as long as they weren't left there overnight; otherwise, they'd be frozen solid in the morning.

The icebox sat in a space as you entered the side door of the house. There were steps on the left that went down to the basement, and on the right, three steps led up to the kitchen. Next to those three steps was a small landing about three feet deep and four feet wide where the ice box sat. It was a necessity during the summer, and my mother was constantly telling us to "close the icebox door: the ice will melt."

Ice delivery was a dying business after the war in the late 1940s and would soon disappear altogether. As a kid, hearing the ice man come down the street was exciting, and my friends and I loved to follow his truck. Once in a while, the ice man let us venture up on the back and look under the tarp that covered the large blocks of ice. We placed our hands on the blocks, and when it was 90 degrees outside, the cold melting ice seeping through our fingers felt wonderful. Those hot, humid summer days in Detroit are vivid memories from another era.

I closed the refrigerator door and turned around to see what was for breakfast before heading off to school. Every so often, breakfast would be a bowl of cereal. If we didn't have any milk, a little water did the trick, or I'd just have it dry. Most days, breakfast was a piece of bread with a little sugar sprinkled on top. To keep the sugar on the bread, I would place it under the faucet and let a few drops of water soak in; too much though, and it would turn soggy. My mother usually told us with confidence, "The sugar bread is good for you. Eat it so you don't get hungry at school." I don't think she really believed that it was good for us, but it was all we had at that time. I often wonder whether all that wheat bread I ate at a young age played any role in my serious wheat allergy that nearly killed me on three occasions years later.

My older brothers, Chuck and Frank, were usually gone before my sisters and I got to the kitchen. Chuck dropped out of high school in the tenth grade. Though my parents were not in favor of it, he wasn't doing well in school and wanted to work. I was surprised because I had never heard of anyone dropping out of school or that it was so easy to do. He worked in a local grocery store until he was eighteen, then got a job at the Cadillac factory in Detroit and was gone every morning by 6 a.m. My other older brother, Frank, was finishing high school. He didn't wait around and was also off to school or work very early every morning.

My sister Marge was married and not living at home any longer but vying for breakfast along with me were my two older sisters, Irene, and Rosemary. Irene didn't have much interest in preparing breakfast and often asked Rosemary to come up with something. Rosemary, from a young age, had a rhythm around the kitchen and was almost as good as my mother at making something out of nothing. She was quick and slammed whatever she could find down on the table saying, "Try this; it's all we have. If you don't like it, you'll go hungry."

As we ate, our mother was moving fast packing lunches, usually baloney sandwiches with mustard. Sometimes my sandwich was wrapped in a Wonder Bread wrapper and then placed in an oversized brown bag. I hated that bread wrapper and pleaded with her to use something else.

"That's all we have," she'd say.

"I have to open that sandwich in the front of all the other kids, and they make fun of me," I complained.

"It's fine. Don't worry about what those kids say. Pay no attention to them. Just open your lunch and eat it." She wiped her hands on her apron and set the bag in front of me on the table, not gently.

I always tried to open my lunch out of view of my friends, or they would point fingers and laugh. "Nice wrapper, Ed. Can't your parents afford to buy waxed paper?" They often said it loudly enough so everyone heard it and it made me feel bad.

My dislike for Cerveny Elementary School began one day in the second grade when I had a temper tantrum and didn't want to go to school. My mother took me by the hand, determined that I go. As we walked past the other kids standing there, I was resisting her hand as she was pulling me forward, and in a loud voice, she said something I will never forget: "Look at Eddie. He doesn't want to go to school. He's acting like a baby." Everyone heard it. I was crushed and embarrassed, trying to hide the tears running down my cheeks.

Another time when I didn't want to go to school, to pacify me, my mother told me she would hand my teacher a note excusing me early to go shopping with her. I sat in class looking out the window, waiting for her to pick me up. The teacher walked over to me and asked what I was looking at, I turned and nervously told her, "I'm waiting to be picked up; I have an excuse to leave early today. My mother said she would give you a note."

"Your mother didn't give me a note," she said. "You have to turn around and pay attention in class."

From then on, I began to distrust more and more what anyone told me, even my friends and family.

Cerveny Elementary School was one very long block from home, and at eight years old, I could walk home for lunch when my mother was there and not at the Federal department store where she worked.

To help pay the bills, she went back to work as a salesperson in the clothing department. It was about two miles from home, and she walked to work, even on cold, snowy winter days, she trudged on. She received employee discounts and first dibs on clothes for us. That meant a lot, and her paycheck also helped with the groceries.

If she were home, I thought maybe I could get out of going back to school for my afternoon classes by trying to look sick and plead with her that I didn't feel well. A couple of times it worked, but she quickly saw through it—especially if all of a sudden, I became miraculously well once it was too late to return—and she didn't hesitate to put me to work.

She was an extremely hard worker, and had a wealth of determination. She rarely rested or took "no" for an answer. In addition to working and running a house, she spent her time crocheting handkerchiefs, doilies, tablecloths, and other things, selling quite a few to her church friends. I was told her crocheting was excellent, but I couldn't tell and didn't care. Sitting there crocheting, she would look at me over the top of her glasses, as I tried to appear sick.

Once, sizing me up, she said, "If you're not going to school, you seem well enough to go door to door in the neighborhood to sell these," and held up a doily she was working on.

I grabbed my stomach and moaned. "I'm not feeling too well. I need to rest."

She set her crochet hooks down, got up, and walked over to where I was lying on the sofa. "Come on. Get up, blondie," she said, taking a gentle hold of my shoulder. "You'll feel better moving around. Let me smooth those pants and straighten out your shirt." She pushed and pulled until my clothes were in line. Reaching for a comb, she ran it through my curly hair a few times. Then, smiling, she added, "There, that's better. You look fine."

I stood there, unenthused about what she wanted me to do—sell her crocheting. She handed me three doilies and three handkerchiefs. I was uncomfortable asking people for money like this. My sisters refused to do it, and since I was the youngest, they'd say, "Let Eddie do it." So, in the early afternoon while other kids were at school, I could be found nervously trying to peddle crochet work in the neighborhood.

Before walking up to knock on the door of a house, I

searched for any sign or excuse for not having to do it. If the window shades were closed, maybe no one was home. If the steps to the porch were cracked, maybe they were too dangerous to walk on. Reluctantly, I slowly made my way to a door and rang the bell. I didn't ring twice.

When someone answered, my sales spiel was, "Do you want to buy a crocheted doily or handkerchief? They are one dollar each or three for two dollars. My mother made them."

The answer was usually, "Tell your mother they are lovely, but no, thank you."

I never liked the sound of saying, "Do you want to buy a doily?" I wasn't even sure what they were for.

One time, someone did buy three handkerchiefs, and I was very proud to take home two dollars. My mother was happy and gave me a big smile. "That's wonderful," she said. I thought I was done for the day, but she had other ideas and told me to try some houses farther down the block on the opposite side of the street. She was never negative, no matter how I did, but if I didn't want to go door to door trying to sell doilies or handkerchiefs anymore, I need to be more creative next time with a more convincing excuse for not going back to school.

School eventually became tolerable. I enjoyed the auditorium. It seemed to be where my imagination flourished with its stage, lights, tall curtains, and rows and rows of seats. It was exciting. We saw movies about places around the world that intrigued me and that I wanted to visit.

For some reason unknown to me, they handed out apples in the auditorium from time to time. That was a treat, as those pieces of bread with sugar and water for breakfast each morning didn't last, and by mid-morning, my stomach was growling as the other kids looked at me.

The school staged a couple of plays in the auditorium, and I was excited by the opportunity to take part in one. I went home and proudly announced, "I am going to be in a school play as an airplane and need to make some wings to wear!"

No one was interested or said anything except my mother. We painted a couple of orange crate boards and tied them to my arms. My role was to fly across the stage as an airplane making airplane noises. I had no idea what the play was about, but I had my fifteen seconds of fame running across that stage.

I also enjoyed planning and building things, and the school's shop class was perfect for that. The teacher, Mr. Stevens, was full of ideas and enthusiastic about teaching us how to actually produce something on our own and take it home as an accomplishment. He thought building a birdhouse would excite the class. It didn't. I was most proud of a hand-carved wooden wall lamp I drew, built, and wired. When I turned it on, it worked, and I felt as bright as that light bulb. I took it home to show everyone. No one said much.

My father, in one of his moods, eventually snarled with discontent, "I hope you don't burn the house down with that damn thing." I thought, *It's not a "damn thing," it's a wall lamp.* I hung that lamp in the basement, longing for some approval from my family. It rarely came, but I was determined not to let that hold me back. I often wished someone at home could feel the excitement and triumph I felt doing things like that.

None of my older brothers and sisters seemed excited about school—their goal was to get out as soon as possible and get a job. My parents came through the Depression when a job was the main objective, so there wasn't any talk about going to college.

No one at home said anything when I proudly announced my achievement of being the best in my math class at a tables competition, meaning I could compute all the mathematical tables—in my head without any writing— faster than anyone else in class.

English classes were sometimes a challenge until I met

Pat Terwilliger. She was a straight-A student and always sat next to me in class because we were seated alphabetically. We struck up a friendship, and during English tests, if I needed a little help with the answers, hers were always conveniently visible on her desk. She was told to cover her work, but that only lasted until the teacher turned around. We really hit it off, and I was happy to see her in and out of school.

Margaret Ferguson was another good friend in school. I had a boyhood crush on her. She always wore a smile, was energetic, athletic, fun to be around, and open to helping me with anything I needed. She lived two blocks away and regularly invited me to her house after school along with a couple of kids to sit around and talk.

It was in the fifth grade during Gym class when a coach invited me to play basketball on a Parks and Recreation team he was coaching at the school at night. I was excited because I had never been asked to play on a team before and was eager to join and learn about basketball. He along with his twin brother, both in their early twenties, coached the team. They were former seminarians, and everyone seemed to like them and think they were cool.

It was going well until one night when the coach was bringing me home from practice. He stopped his car on a dark street a few blocks from my house, turning the engine and lights off. He started telling me how my play on the team was improving, and then he reached over, put his hand into my pants, and began fondling me.

I didn't know what it was all about and said, "I don't want you to do that. I want to go home."

He stopped. "Are you sure?" he asked.

Shaking, afraid, and almost crying, I said, "Yes, I want to go home!"

He started the car and took me home, warning me, "Don't tell anyone about this."

I never went back to the team. My mother and brothers

asked why, and I simply said, "Practicing at night is tiring, and it wasn't fun anymore." Those were lies. I had been having a great time until that night. Many years later, I heard a rumor that the coach was arrested on child molestation charges. With him being a former seminarian, it drew wide media attention.

Succeeding in school with little support from home was nearly impossible, as my home environment didn't lend itself to saying "Hoorah!" for academia. Getting to school with dry feet was always a challenge, too. Being the youngest at the time, I had hand-me-down shoes from my older brothers, and they had a great deal of wear and tear. The heels were worn down, and the soles usually had holes in them. Placing a piece of stiff cardboard in the shoes to seal the holes, I could feel the bounce in my step and thought, *this must be how the other kids feel in their shoes that don't have holes in them.* My friends were sometimes cruel, and I was singled out as being too poor to afford good shoes.

They would laugh and scream, "Hey Ed, you've got holes in your shoes. Can't your parents buy you better shoes?" It was humiliating.

My father didn't seem concerned about my shoes—or anything in my world at the time, for that matter. He was oblivious to how I was doing in school and never asked anything about it. We ate dinner when he came home from work, then he'd read the newspaper, listen to the news on the radio, and usually fall asleep in his chair, wake up, and go upstairs to bed. We eventually got a TV, and he did the same thing, just replacing the radio with TV.

If he came home from work late, he would have dinner by himself in the small kitchen at the white-painted kitchen table. It had three matching wooden chairs, one of which always seemed to be broken. My father was usually grumpy and tired, alone reading the newspaper. Sitting in the kitchen, he could see the side door leading outside and it provided him the opportunity to scream at anyone who didn't close that door quickly enough. He would look up and holler, "Close that damn door, you're letting all the heat out." I was fearful he would explode even more if I said anything, so I closed the door and quickly moved through the kitchen trying to avoid him during those times. My brothers and sisters knew better than to bother him, too, but they seemed much less fazed than I was by his indifference about our lives.

Perhaps if he had shown more interest, it would have helped us all.

CHAPTER 3

O n those gray winter mornings when the Michigan temperatures sank to the low teens—and sometimes zero or below—it was tense around the house as we scrambled to stay warm.

We had an old coal-burning furnace in the basement and I could tell by the thin layer of ice on the storm windows that the fire from the night before had gone out. My father would leave for work at the Ford factory around 6:00 each morning. Once in a while, he would go to the basement before leaving to stoke the furnace's ashes and see if they would ignite. They rarely did. He would slam the iron furnace door shut with a loud *clank* and simply head off to work, knowing my mother would deal with it.

Shortly after he left, in her pajamas, robe, and slippers, my mother would trudge down into the freezing basement to get a fire going before the rest of us woke up. She would gather whatever wood scraps and paper were there, and once it started burning, she would add some coal if there was any. We were often out of coal during the winter. Even though the coal bin held a full ton, we didn't have the money to keep it filled—usually only enough to buy a quarter ton—so sometimes we only had wood.

In the winter, it was my job to gather wood for the furnace after school each day, so I'd go through the alleys behind the local grocery stores to search for empty wooden crates to bring home. Sometimes, the crates were laden with bugs scavenging the last pieces of leftover fruit on the wood. I'd swat them off and load the crates onto my bike. I also looked for new houses being built in the neighborhood to collect any wood scraps lying around. At times, I felt like a thief picking up those pieces of wood.

My friends quickly gave me the nickname "Woodchuck".

"Hey, Ed! Woodchuck, chuck, chuck!" they hollered and laughed when they saw me with a pile of boxes and scrap wood tediously balanced on the front of my bike. It was humiliating, as if they were laughing at my entire family. Sometimes they tried to knock me over as I passed them.

When the fire in the furnace finally began, my sisters and I would jump out of bed and hug a heat register to absorb any of its first traces of heat.

"It's cold!" we often screamed.

"Get up and move around. You'll warm up faster," my mother screamed back, making as much noise as she possibly could to wake us. The chilly air kept us moving quickly as we hurried down to the kitchen to soak in some additional warmth from the stove that was on before heading off to school.

At one time, there were as many as nine people living in our house, with my two brothers and me sharing a bed in one bedroom. I was either squashed between them or one of them would turn in the opposite direction, his feet in my face. Despite that, it gave me a secure feeling to be with my brothers. My three sisters shared a bed in another bedroom, and my parents and grandmother took the last two rooms.

My oldest sister, Marge, moved out when she married an Air Force officer soon after World War II ended. Marge was pretty enough to be a model on the cover of a magazine. She was slender, carried herself straight and tall, had long, dark hair and large, dark eyes. Her smile was wide and full, and her charismatic enthusiasm drew people to her. She and her new husband, Bert, were lucky enough to get into housing the military had constructed for returning servicemen near downtown Detroit. I was standing with them once when he was in his Air Force uniform, all neat and clean looking. I saw a scar on his left hand.

"What's that?" I asked in wonderment.

"I was shot in the hand flying a plane in the war-"

And before he could finish his story, my sister jumped in, "Bert, stop telling him those stories. You weren't shot. Eddie, don't believe him."

I didn't know whom to believe, and Bert always seemed to embellish his "stories," but I enjoyed listening to them.

It took a long time before my father accepted Bert. He may have resented the man because Bert had a white-collar job in the "Glass House," Ford's world headquarters in Dearborn, while my father worked in one of the factories. Or maybe he just didn't feel Bert was good enough for his favorite daughter.

A year after Marge and Bert were married, my younger brother, Less, was born. I wasn't sure my parents wanted child number seven since they were both in their forties by then. Now, there would be four boys in one bedroom.

It seemed so loud and chaotic at home. My older brothers were telling me one thing, my sisters pushed for something else, and my parents continuously tried to maintain some control telling me something completely different. The whole while, I was merely attempting to make sense of it all.

Who is in charge? Whom do I listen to? Whom do I follow?

During all of this commotion and conflict, I often wanted to simply get away to a quiet respite, telling myself it would all pass. I took refuge sometimes outside on the front porch. Our two-story brick house, like many homes in the neighborhood, had a porch that became the center of activity during those warm, humid summer days and evenings as passersby said, "Hello."

In the silence of twilight, I took in the smell of freshly cut grass from earlier in the day, and I could still feel the afternoon warmth on the porch concrete while lying there listening to the crickets announce their presence and watching the fireflies perform their dance in the darkened sky. Their tiny sparkling glimmers moved freely in no set pattern. I wondered: *Is it possible to reach out for a firefly to feel it fly through my fingers? Maybe if I stood on a ladder or climbed up a tree, I could extend my reach and possibly grasp one, even if only for a moment.*

I gazed at the stars and fireflies, dreaming of where I wanted to go and things I wanted to do. I always felt there was someplace better than where I was.

The stillness was occasionally broken by a passing car with its convertible top down and the sound of laughter and music filling the air.

Sometimes, that car was driven by one of the neighbors' oldest boys. The McIlrath's—an Irish family with six kids—lived next door to us. Mr. McIlrath was a brick layer, born in Ireland, and he used to play soccer there.

He was always kicking a ball, bragging in a thick Irish brogue, "Eddie, come on over! Let me show you how to play soccer and how we played it back home." His accent was so strong that sometimes I had no idea what he was saying.

With so many kids between our two houses, there were few quiet moments. My three sisters and the three McIlrath girls were constantly going back and forth. To add more confusion, we couldn't afford a phone and had to go either to the next-door neighbor Dobson's or to the McIlrath's to make a call. Having a private phone was expensive. Eventually, we got a party line with the McIlraths to share costs, and I always found it awkward to hear someone already talking on the party line when lifting the receiver off the hook.

I saw my mother carefully pick up the receiver several times and heard her say, sounding very friendly, "Will you be long? OK, thank you."

I was curious and gave it a try. The minute I lifted the receiver, the McIlrath girls heard it click and laid into me screaming, "Get the hell off the line! Can't you hear we're talking?"

I didn't make that mistake again and quickly learned that if you're really quiet, it *might* be possible to lift the receiver without hearing a click. Finally, we got a private line, but it was often shut off from the bill going unpaid. My sisters were furious when that happened, but it didn't bother me because I never used the phone anyway.

My Hungarian grandmother, Jolan, lived with us and had the fourth bedroom. She didn't speak much English around the house, other than cuss words she heard my father use. She and my mother conversed in some Hungarian, and of course, my father spoke Hungarian. Because she rarely spoke English, she seemed to make things more difficult for everyone. She often said things to me in Hungarian that I didn't understand. Passing her bedroom, if I got the nerve to go in, she would pat me on the head, smile, and whisper in Hungarian, *"Édes Kisfiú,"* and give me a nickel or a dime— or sometimes, even a quarter. I didn't know what *'Edes Kisfiú'* meant at the time but learned later that it means "sweet little boy." If I had known it then, maybe I would have gone into her room more often hoping for some more money.

I took the money she gave me and usually ran down to the small corner market to buy some candy, especially Milk Duds and those long strips of colored dots. It was a family market, serving mainly the neighbors from several surrounding blocks. If you didn't have enough to pay for something, Mr. Armenio, the owner, trusted most regulars who came in and would jot the amount next to your name in a small book he kept under the counter. *Twenty-five cents, Mrs. Tar, Bread.* You paid him later. The market's selection was limited to essentials like fruits, vegetables, bread, milk, and a small meat counter. It had a center isle containing canned goods, cereal, soup and the like.

One day, going in for a piece of candy, I couldn't resist looking at those large red apples. I was famished. When Mr. Armenio wasn't looking, I took an apple and stuffed it into my pants. I tried to look nonchalant as I walked through the store toward the exit, and the apple rolled down my pant leg onto the floor. A lady coming toward me in the aisle was startled and raised her eyebrows when the apple suddenly appeared.

I looked at her nervously, and to defend what had just happened, said something really dumb, "Oh, this apple must have fallen out of one of these cans."

She gazed at me for a moment with a wrinkled forehead, and said nothing as I picked up the apple, placed it on the shelf next to a can, and began quickly walking out of the store. She gave me a wink and a slight smile as I left. Fearing she would tell Mr. Armenio, who would tell my mother or jot it in his book, I didn't go back to the store for a very long time. After that, I never attempted to steal another red apple—or any apple—anywhere.

My grandmother had some money and loaned my parents $3,700 in 1937 to buy the house where I was born on Mark Twain Street. I don't think they paid off that loan, though. I believe it was in exchange for allowing her to live there. She was sixty-four years old at the time and had been married three times. No one ever really said how she came up with the money. There was the sense that she was "hoarding" more somewhere in her room, possibly in a wall panel or sewn into her mattress.

My mother was always urging my father to ask her where she hid the money.

He'd say, "I *did* ask her. She doesn't have any money."

"I don't believe that. Ask her again."

Before long, a full-blown argument would erupt between my parents, with my father freely using cuss words or some disparaging remarks as the squabble deteriorated into something completely different than what it had initially been about.

When my grandmother died, I felt a little emptiness as she had always been around with a smile and word or two for me. Even though I didn't understand what she was saying, I sensed she was always on my side. I was sad she was gone.

After her death, her bedroom was turned upside down and the mattress cut open in the quest for money. Nothing was ever found, and it became a discussion point for years, with accusations that someone in the family had slowly taken my grandmother's money and my sister Marge had helped herself to some of the jewelry that disappeared when she died.

During all the upheaval of living in a crowded house, that one bathroom we had—with no working shower—added to the stress. Something had to be done. My brother Chuck finally rigged a shower in the basement, but my sisters were the only ones who went down there to use it. I don't know how they could stand it in the basement. It was messy and dirty from the coal-burning furnace, a coal bin, stacks of newspapers, wood, an old washing machine with a hand wringer and a couple of sinks my mother used when she was canning our fruits and vegetables.

In the empty lot next to our house, we kept a garden where we grew tomatoes, cucumbers, peppers, and a few other things. We also had a peach tree and a not-so-healthy, dying, apple tree. My mother spent many hours in the basement canning. She scrubbed the old mason jars that had been saved from last season, replaced the lids' worn-out rubber washers, and then packed the jars with the fruits and vegetables she just cleaned from our garden. Firmly tightening the lids, she would hand them to me one at a time saying, "Be careful and put these in the storage room. Be sure they are not on the edge of the shelves so they won't fall off." The canned fruit and vegetables were used during the winter months.

Those basement sinks were also used to drain the blood from the chickens we raised in our yard. On special occasions—Easter, Thanksgiving, and Christmas—one of the chickens was the lucky winner to be selected for dinner.

My mother would pick out a chicken, bring it into the basement, and say, "Stand back," as I watched her take hold of the chicken's neck and twist it. The chicken would let out a loud shriek, and it was over. She then soaked it in scalding-hot water to soften and loosen the feathers that I would sometimes pluck.

Then she cut it open and cleaned out the insides. I was allowed to singe off the short stubby feathers, over the stove upstairs in the kitchen, as she blurted out instructions while standing there to make sure I didn't burn the raw chicken. She was ready to take hold of it if needed, but she usually gave me the freedom to do it myself.

"Hold on to it tight. Ok, turn it… Careful… Not too close… Don't burn it… Careful. It looks good, that's enough."

I enjoyed doing that. She was quick to laugh and didn't seem to take it too seriously if I held the chicken over the flame too long in one position. Smiling, with no anger in her voice, she would say, "That piece will be a bit more well done." Then with a wink and a secretive whisper, "We'll give that piece to one of your brothers to eat." It made me feel important to be doing something alone with her, without my brothers and sisters there demanding her attention. I knew she would brag about how well I did.

We had rabbits, too, but we eventually got rid of them as they multiplied very rapidly, and we also stopped raising chickens. It was a real mess trying to keep all those cages clean and the rats away.

The rats roamed the alleys looking for food and bored holes through the dirt floor into our garage. They were always hanging around, maybe eyeing the chicken food we kept in there. The garage was wooden and old with a leaking roof in places. It had a dark, musty smell from the damp dirt floor, oil rags, empty oil cans, car grease, and an assortment of junk.

My father kept the family car on one side. During the war, he had a black four-door 1940 Packard and used ration stamps to buy gas. Now, as the 40s came to an end, he had a later version of the same car. It seemed to run well without major problems as he always seemed to be tinkering with it.

Once, I went in the garage while he was under the hood of the car, and I heard a scurrying in the corner. I asked what the noise was. Without looking up, he roared, "It's those goddamn rats—they're back. Stay the hell away from them."

How was I supposed to do that with our wagon, sled, bikes, and other things in there?

It was a little scary to hear the skittering of the rats when I opened the large, wobbly garage doors. I said to him, "The entire garage could be cleaned, then maybe the rats won't come back." He grunted but didn't say anything.

No one showed any interest in cleaning it out—they thought it was a frivolous idea. I decided to slowly begin removing some of the trash lying around. There was an old bent bike frame, broken pieces of fence, rusting wheels, mildewed and stinking old clothes, a broken window frame, papers, broken pieces of bricks, old shovels, chicken wire, bottles...

When I moved something, the rats moved. I always made sure I had a shovel within arm's reach to crush any rat that happened to make a run for it. The rats were as scared as I was, so once I realized that, it wasn't too bad—unless they made a beeline directly toward me. I either stood my ground and whacked them or turned and ran outside.

My father and brothers said I was wasting my time and offered no help except to tell me what not to throw out (which was nearly everything). I just kept moving forward, trying to ignore them.

Looking up from working on the car, he would mutter, "Do you even know what the hell you're doing, kid?"

Chuck, often sounding disinterested, would say, "Why are you wasting your time doing that? Those rats will just come back."

Rosemary would add that I was crazy. "One of those rats is going to bite you and then you'll stop trying to clean it up."

My father seemed to put down whatever I was doing. "Crazy kid," he'd say. "Get the out of here." At least my mother was somewhat encouraging, telling me to be careful and do what I thought needed to be done.

I continued to slowly clean it up. When it was done, everyone seemed happy with it and for the first time ever, could use both sides of the garage to park a car if needed. And the rats did not return.

Sometimes standing in the yard, I could look in the rear dining room window and see the activity inside and hear the arguing. Rather than going in, I would often just walk over to a friend's house two doors away. I didn't go to the McIlraths right next door because they probably heard the arguing too, and that was embarrassing.

Our other neighbor, the Dobsons, appeared to me to be the ideal family. I never heard an argument or anyone raise their voice. Mr. Dobson liked to sit and smoke his pipe, read the paper, and watch TV. If anyone asked him a question, he would answer, almost sounding like a school teacher, with a calming voice that would assure us that his answers were correct. He seemed to know just about everything. He insisted we call him by his first name, George, and I felt a little strange about that as all the kids I knew called adults by their last name only with a Mr. or Mrs. in front of it.

When black-and-white TVs came out, they were the first on the street to have one. I was at their house as much as possible watching TV and was especially intrigued by how the news was presented by *Douglas Edwards with the News* on CBS and *The Camel News Caravan* with John Cameron Swayze on NBC.

Those shows made a lasting impression on me and gave me a glimpse at places and activities around the world that I dreamed of visiting one day. The popular kids' shows at the time such as *Kukla, Fran and Ollie* and *Howdy Doody* were not for me. We didn't get a TV in our house until a couple of years later.

My mother and Ann Dobson were very close, so she knew what my mother was going through with my father's outrageous arguments. My father, on the other hand, didn't like that I was at the Dobson's so often and didn't hesitate to let me know, yelling,

"Why the hell are you there so much? Get home: they don't want you there."

I said, "I like to watch the TV shows. They don't mind if I am there."

He would explode, "Yes, they do. Get home!"

His words put doubts in my mind. Whenever the Dobson's asked me to stay for dinner, I often doubted they meant it, hearing those words ringing in my ear: "They don't really want you there." Once, I did accept their offer but felt uneasy fearing my father's ranting when I got home. My mother knew I had stayed for dinner, probably my father did too, but he said nothing.

I had many friends on the block and began thinking— whenever I was at one of their houses—that maybe they didn't want me there, either. I couldn't escape those words.

They had a profound effect on me, no matter where I was. "They don't want you there."

CHAPTER 4

We were raised Catholic. To fully participate in the religion, we had to receive the sacrament of Holy Communion.

My oldest sister Marge and younger brother Les were the only ones to attend a Catholic school for a couple of semesters, where preparation classes for First Communion were part of the curriculum. My parents didn't have the money to send anyone else, so my two other brothers, my two other sisters, and me had to attend preparation classes on Saturday mornings at the nearby Catholic school.

The school was about a two-mile walk and sat across the street from a large, intimidating Catholic church with high spires, crosses, and statues of the saints looking down as if they were judging everyone walking by. It was named Precious Blood Parish. I didn't know how the names of parishes were chosen, but that sounded somewhat ghoulish to me, a nine-year-old kid.

That First Communion journey was a real adventure. My sister Rosemary, three years older, also had to attend the same class as me, and we walked together each Saturday. My mother gave her the responsibility of making sure I got there and back safely. Of course, always the rebel, Rosemary had her own ideas about attending class.

The first time we skipped class, Rosemary dismissed my concerns. She told me with her trademark aplomb, "Today's class is not important; we don't need to go."

I was surprised, as I had never cut any class anywhere.

"We'll get into trouble," I said. "We have to go."

Turning and walking toward a drug store, she replied, "You can go if you want, but I am not going." I gave in, and she assured me everything would be all right.

At her cajoling, rather than going to class every week, we spent a good amount of time at the soda fountain of the nearby Cunningham's Drug Store drinking a soda or walking around the F.W. Woolworth five-and-dime near the school. I was always afraid someone would report us, even though no one knew who we were and probably didn't care one way or the other—unless it was a nun from the school.

In class, the nuns peered at us with eyes like lasers, and those long habits they wore surely didn't help their visage. I withdrew as much as possible so they wouldn't call on me to recite a prayer or criticize me about something I didn't know.

Rosemary always had answers, especially when we got home and our mother would ask questions,

"How was class today?"

"Oh, fine. We're learning a lot."

"Tell me about it, like what," my mother usually probed.

Rosemary, rushing and trying to avoid answering, said, "I'll tell you later. I have to go. My friends are outside."

I always walked away when that conversation began so I wouldn't be asked.

We skipped about every third class. When we did go, the nuns would ask us where we had been the previous week, to which Rosemary would smile and give her standard answer:

"Oh, uh… we were sick," or "We had to go somewhere

with our mother."

One time, when Rosemary cut a class, I decided I wasn't going to and the nun became suspicious. She asked me where Rosemary was, and I found myself fumbling for an answer. That's when the nun called our mother. I wasn't very good at making up even the simplest excuse like "I don't know."

Despite being pressured to ditch with my sister periodically, I took the classes seriously and would lie in bed at home, sometimes under the covers with a flashlight, trying to memorize the prayers I might be asked to recite the following week.

After a semester of Saturday classes, we were ready to make our first confession the day before our First Communion. That first confession remains vivid in my mind.

The nuns lined us up and led us into the large, empty church where we knelt in the pews near the confessional. I was nervous and had little idea of what to do in confession since most of that had been covered in one of the classes we'd skipped. I was struggling to remember when the confessional's curtain opened and the kid before me came out. It was my turn. I got up, stepped toward the confessional, pulled the curtain back, stepped in, and closed the curtain.

The confessional was the size of a small closet. It was dark, stuffy, and smelled very old. I knelt on the kneeler and looked straight ahead into the wall, then I heard the small slot in the wall—about a foot wide—open. I couldn't see the priest, as the opening was covered with a dark screen. As I knelt there, trembling a bit, the priest mumbled something I couldn't understand.

Then he said, "OK, begin."

I froze, kneeling in silence, not knowing what I was supposed to do.

There was a pause, and he said again, "OK, begin."

I didn't do anything.

He asked, "Do you know the how to make a confession?"

"Uh… no, I don't think so," I whispered, shaking.

"OK, start with 'Bless me, Father, for I have sinned'."

I repeated that.

"Now, what sins have you committed?"

I didn't know if I had committed any sins—I was only nine years old.

Thoughts kept running through my mind: *What if someone in the pews on the other side of the curtain is listening? Can they hear me? Should I make something up?*

The priest asked me again, "Do you have any sins to confess?"

"I don't think so," I answered.

"Have you ever said any bad words to anyone?"

"I don't think I have."

"Have you ever been mad at anyone?"

I stuttered a little, "Y-yes, I was mad at my friend once."

"Anything else?"

I said, "No. That's all I can remember."

"OK. Try not to get mad at anyone and make an act of contrition."

I didn't know how to say an act of contrition, and he slowly had me repeat it after him.

At the end, he was mumbling again, and then said, "As your penance, say two Hail Marys."

I heard the little window close.

I knelt there for several seconds, as I wasn't sure if it would open again, then I got up, parted the curtain, went back to the pew, and it was the next kid's turn. It smelled better in the church. I tried to relax for the first time that morning and quickly said two Hail Mary prayers. I was relieved it was over and felt proud of myself for having weathered that experience.

I wondered what the priest thought of the classroom

nuns when I told him I had no idea what to do in confession. Did he really care? The priest seemed to have a little more compassion than the nuns who probably would have thought "getting mad at a friend" was simply terrible.

Rosemary never mentioned her confession experience, and I was afraid to ask because I didn't want her to ask about mine. I wondered: *had she gone through the same thing I had?*

We were not allowed to eat from midnight Saturday until after First Communion at Mass Sunday morning. I thought it was a dumb rule, but the nuns put the fear of God in us about sinning and going to Hell if we broke it. I really had no idea what would happen, but our mother wouldn't bend.

Church rules change. Do the poor souls who violated those silly outdated rules really go to Hell? And if so, were they released after the Church changed its rules?

Even before making our first communion, my mother always attempted, sometimes successfully, to drag at least one of us kids to Mass every Sunday. I could see how proud she was, walking into church. No one really wanted to go. My older brothers and sisters always had an excuse. That left me. I never felt I belonged there with all those kids who attended Catholic school every day.

The pastor at Precious Blood Parish, Monsignor Hermes, wouldn't hesitate to stop his sermon midway through, and from the pulpit, raise his voice, and point out someone who was coming in late. He would shout, "Mass started at 9 a.m. If you can't be here on time, maybe you shouldn't come at all, or go to some other Mass or another church." Sometimes he called out their name. That shocked me, and I decided right then that if I was going to go to church, I had better not be late.

Sunday morning—the day we were making our first communion — was very hot, and the church was packed with people waving fans, trying to stay cool. Sitting there along with countless other kids from various classes, the Mass seemed to take forever, I was so hungry that I got dizzy and nearly passed out from not eating.

After receiving First Communion, we finally headed home for food and pictures. Our entire family was there along with aunts and uncles. We rarely got any new clothes, but our mother bought a new white communion dress for Rosemary and for me, new white pants, a white shirt and tie, and for the first time, new shoes. There were no holes or cardboard in the soles this time.

Uncle Joe was his usual self. "Eddie boy, you look good today," he said, and that made me feel special. He always had a positive demeanor when he came over to our house. He seemed to enjoy himself and wanted others around him to enjoy themselves too—it was infectious. He was full of ideas for doing something fun like when my parents celebrated their 25th wedding anniversary and we had a large celebration in our house. It was full with people and the party was brimming and boisterous.

Family pictures were being taken, so everyone was in dressy clothes: suits, ties, and dresses. I had never seen my brothers and sisters and parents all dressed up at the same time. I wore a casual shirt and pants, as did my three-year-old brother, Les. My sister Marge lit up the picture with her bright smile.

After the pictures, standing in the crowded living room, Uncle Joe decided to take things into his own hands. He was my mother's favorite brother—a former Golden Gloves boxer, standing nearly six feet tall with broad shoulders. He would have made a good bouncer in a rowdy bar. Wearing an enormous smile, he always walked into a room happy and triumphant. He was a character just looking for a good time and his enthusiasm was contagious.

He buttoned up the collar on his white shirt, and turned his dark suit jacket around to look like a priest. In his big, preacher-style voice, he quickly called everyone together for a special event.

He had my parents hold hands and shouted loudly enough for the neighbors to hear, "I am about to have Rose and Lou renew their marriage vows!"

Everyone cheered.

He grabbed a book off a nearby table to use as the vow book from which he was supposedly reading his version of the marriage vows.

He began, "Everyone now, can I get an *amen.*"

"Amen!" they shouted with some laughter.

With his resounding voice, he said, "OK, Louis—better known as Lou—do you promise to have a good time with Rose till death do you part?"

My father actually reacted and smiled, "I hope so."

Uncle Joe continued, "Rose, do you promise to have a good time with Lou till death do you part?"

My mother broke out laughing. "I'll try," she said.

Everyone laughed, but not breaking character, Uncle Joe continued, "'Try'? Rose, *try* isn't good enough. We cannot accept that or any ifs, ands, or buts. It has to be either 'Yes' or 'No'."

"OK, yes," my mother said between laughs.

Uncle Joe asked for another *amen* and said, "By the power invested in me by the Almighty," everyone laughed, "and my own power as Joe Schultz, brother of Rose and brother-in-law of Lou, this marriage is now officially renewed for at least another 25 years... and longer if you play your cards right. OK, Lou, give her a big kiss to seal the deal."

That was a warm moment, as I had never seen them kiss before.

Uncle Joe continued, "Now, everyone, join me in singing the *Anniversary Song* for Rose and Lou."

They began, "Oh how they danced on the night they were wed..."

It was one of the rare times I saw my parents relaxed

and happy at the same time. There were cheers and another "Amen!" with everyone laughing and having a great time. Only Uncle Joe could pull that off.

Down in the basement, the party continued, with music playing on the record changer that had replaced the old Victrola. There was dancing and singing. Two boards were placed over the laundry sinks to create a bar. Cases of beer were stacked on the floor, and glasses were on top of the bar along with 7 Up, Vernor's ginger ale, Coke, and a few liquor bottles.

I heard my Uncle Jim say to whoever was pouring liquor, "I'll take another shot of that Seven Crown."

Someone also asked for a "Seven and Seven." I wasn't sure what Seven Crown or a Seven and Seven was, but I heard it a few more times. The food was spread out upstairs on the dining room table. I probably wore out those basement steps running up and down, trying to take it all in. It was exciting.

As it got late and the party rolled on, it suddenly changed. I heard screams and loud female voices followed by a crash of chairs. My mother's two sisters, Aunt Annie, who always seemed quiet and meek, and Aunt Eleanor, who was the polar opposite, were rolling in a full fight on the hard concrete basement floor, scratching and pulling each other's hair. I didn't see all of it, as everyone quickly surrounded them, pulling them apart. I had never seen two grown women fight before and had no idea what it was about. It was messy and loud.

My aunts didn't speak to each other for years after that. And although my mother made a great effort for them to reconcile. I don't think they really ever did.

Most of my uncles were tethered together by jobs in or around the auto industry, and they often came to our house to play poker on weekends. The talk around the table usually centered on events and activities "in the plant," where they worked and which they knew so well. The atmosphere was convivial and relaxed at the large dining room table as they opened the deck of playing cards. I had no fear of being screamed at or having negative comments directed at me—which happened so often by my father in our daily home life—so I stayed and watched as late as I could. I often glanced at my father and hoped he wouldn't have another epileptic seizure.

Uncle Joe worked at GM. He always spoke with bravado and in a magnanimous voice. "Eddie boy, come on, let's sing," he'd say and then break into *Danny Boy*, which always seemed to be at the top of his song list.

In addition to bragging about his former boxing conquests, he also had kind words for the fighters who beat him. "That guy had big mitts and knew how to use 'em," he said, describing getting knocked out once. I liked hearing his stories, though my other uncles sometimes had doubts about what he was saying.

Uncle Jim—who was married to one of my mother's sisters—was self-employed and operated his own Timken tool route. He was freewheeling, always seemed happy, always positive, and a bit mysterious. Rumor was he had a steady lady friend despite being married to my aunt. With a cigarette hanging from his lips, he looked like a gambler from the 1930s with his thin mustache, chiseled face, and the ever-present mischievous smile. His stories fascinated me. His attitude seemed to be, "Don't worry, enjoy yourself," and he did.

Those Saturday night card games were fun for me. I was always singled out by one of my uncles and asked to give advice on how much to bet as they showed me their cards.

"I don't know, maybe ten cents," I'd say.

They would then sometimes respond, "How about we bet twenty cents?"

I quickly agreed and watched the pot grow larger. And if they won, they would always slip me some money for my "advice". I saved that money so I could go to the movies the next Saturday morning.

There was no shortage of complaining about work around the table.

Pulling a fresh toothpick out of his shirt pocket and placing it in the side of his mouth (my father always seemed to have a toothpick in his mouth), said, "Those sons of bitches in the plant want me to stay away from the line and work in paint and maintenance. Bastards!"

My mother heard him. "Don't use that language. The kids are around."

"Oh, they've heard worse than that."

Actually, that was mild compared to what he usually said around the house. His comments opened up a variety of responses from my uncles.

"I wouldn't hesitate to go to the union steward," Uncle Ed said. Then he folded his hand and threw cards to the center of the table. He worked at Dodge.

"File a complaint," Uncle Joe quickly interjected.

Uncle Dan, who was the quiet one among my uncles added, as he carefully studied his cards, "They only have your best interest in mind, Lou."

Uncle Jim had a different idea.

"Lou, why the hell don't you quit and get a job at a small auto shop? You know more about cars than anyone, and you could call your own shots. You'll still be eligible for your pension from Ford. There are shops along Livernois—near the plant—that could use someone like you. I deliver tools to most of them and could help you if you want."

"Hell no!" my father quickly said. "Some of those guys are crooks who don't know much about cars."

"That's the point, Lou, you do," Uncle Jim replied.

The conversation continued, but my father rarely took their suggestions.

My mother, always listening, knew about the auto industry, having worked in it years before. She often reminded my father about my uncles' suggestions, and he'd become upset when she prodded him about it.

I loved when my aunts and uncles came over because it meant I could stay up later while they were there and take part in the fun. At times I felt disconnected with all the activity at home, but not on these nights. They were exactly what I hoped they would be—a happy gathering of my extended family. It was hectic, and I devoured the joy of it all.

CHAPTER 5

G rowing up in a large family in a very crowded house, there was never a dull moment.

One time, Frank and Chuck were arguing, and Frank had a pair of scissors in his hands. He swung the scissors and almost nicked Chuck in his chest. My mother saw it, leaped between them, and screamed, "What are you doing, Frank? Holy Mary, Mother of God—you could have killed him!" I wasn't sure whether he meant to swing those scissors or not, but after that incident, I was always careful around Frank. You never knew what he would do.

Frank was a couple of years younger than Chuck and had a reputation as a hothead. He was stocky, wore his hair in a crew cut, had an easy smile and a confident walk. Maybe he felt like he had to act tough because he wasn't very tall. He was loud and bragged, always acting like he knew everything, and he rarely backed down when challenged.

Chuck, on the other hand, projected stillness. To me he seemed more level-headed and consistent than Frank. Over six feet tall and broad-shouldered, he served as an MP in the army, and didn't have to prove his toughness. He had a long stride and always stood tall with his chest out. He answered questions confidently, but he also had a habit of nervously clearing his throat.

It was Chuck who guided the family through the rough times when my father failed to bring home a paycheck. One night, he gathered everyone in the living room and laid out a plan for paying the overdue bills, which were mounting up. My two brothers and two sisters were still living at home and working. And Chuck wanted everyone to pay a small amount every month for room and board. The tension was thick as he stood in the middle of the room, explaining what seemed to be a perfect solution to a serious problem. He helped the family a lot since he started working at Cadillac factory a few years earlier.

My father, sitting in his favorite chair, began to sizzle, shaking his head from side to side. He grumbled, "I make enough to pay the goddamn bills and don't need your help."

My mother looked at my father, and snapped, "Yes, but you only bring home a few dollars each week and gamble the rest away. What am I supposed to do with that?"

Heatedly, my father replied, "It's enough to pay the damn bills!"

"No, it's not!"

Chuck interrupted, sounding a bit irritated himself. "Look, let's not get into an argument. This is the only way to make ends meet right now. Once we're caught up on all the bills, we can stop it."

He held up a handful of papers. "Here are the overdue bills, including the house payments. The house is close to foreclosure."

My sister Irene stood in the corner, her arms folded across her chest, looking a little bored, she sighed, "It's not my job to pay the bills. I'm not paying anything."

"You live here," Chuck responded, "and you can help out."

Rosemary sat on a chair looking impatient, one leg bouncing up and down in constant motion. She stood up and moved toward the door. "If Irene isn't paying, I'm not paying anything either. I work my rear end off cleaning the house and doing everything no one else wants to do around here. That's my contribution."

Frank didn't want to pay either. Leaning against a wall, he finally said, "Daddy has to bring home a full paycheck."

My father bristled at that shouting, "What the hell? You are going to tell me what I have to bring home? This is my house!"

I sat taking it all in, and couldn't understand why they were fighting about working together to solve a problem that affected us all.

Irene said, "I've got to go." She went upstairs to get ready to go out that evening. Then Rosemary walked out. My brothers were left talking with my father, who looked like he wanted none of it.

Eventually, Chuck, with some help from Marge's husband Bert, managed to get caught up on the house payments so the bank wouldn't foreclose. Chuck said he felt like the "fall guy" around the house as he was blamed for everything that went wrong.

The phone company turned off the phone several more times. The electric company threatened to turn off the power, and my mother was constantly on the phone with the bank, pleading for more time to make the house payments.

My father always seemed uncomfortable when confronted with the fact that we lacked the money to pay the utility bills and the house payment, let alone enough to fill the refrigerator with food. He often blurted out something about my mother's inability to handle the money correctly, hollering, "You waste the money I bring home. I bring home enough money!" Then he would start verbally abusing her, making disparaging remarks and accusing her of lying.

Maybe it was because I was younger than my siblings, but his cruelty to her seemed to affect me more than the others. I tried to withdraw as my mother pleaded with him, "Stop all the filthy language and ranting in front of the kids!"

During their loudest arguments, my foul-mouthed father accused my mother of infidelity in graphic language. In tears, my mother told me, "Eddie, go outside; you shouldn't be hearing this." I thought... *If only I could escape from all of this.*

But whenever my father won some money betting on the horses, there was less arguing. My mother was happier those nights, and my father might even crack a smile. Once, I asked my mother, "Where did the extra money come from for all these groceries?"

She brushed it off. "Your father worked extra this week."

Many things that happened at home seemed to be a secret and were kept from me. I had to fill in the blanks myself.

My sister Irene, dropped out of school as soon as she was old enough and although she didn't like the yelling and verbal abuse our father flung around, she usually sided with him against my mother. That confused me.

Beginning in her late teens, it seemed as though whenever I walked through the living room, Irene would be sitting on the couch, prepping for an evening out. She looked so self-assured, sitting there, polishing her long fingernails, a burning cigarette balanced on the edge of a nearby ashtray. Her large brown eyes were steady and focused as she worked on her nails; her legs were usually stretched out in front of her with matching polish drying on her toenails.

Without any makeup, her nondescript blouse and worn-out shorts made her look plain and rather drab. The large white curlers in her hair resembled a pile of three-inch white PVC pipes.

If she had something to say to me, she would set the polish down, glance up, reach for the cigarette, take a long, slow drag, tilt her head back slightly, purse her lips, and slowly blow the smoke into the air, and then she would start to talk. I knew all her moves.

When asked to help around the house, her responses were direct. "I don't do those kinds of things. That's for someone else to do." She didn't seem to care what anyone thought; she knew what she was about, and that was it. Irene spoke with confidence and moved at her own speed, on her own terms.

I always got along with her, but also knew when to keep my distance. Later in life, she became the person in the family whom everyone respected and went to for sage advice. Everyone loved to spend time with her.

My sister Rosemary also dropped out of high school and had many contentious arguments with my parents, who wanted her to stay in school. Then one day when she was sixteen, she simply stopped going. My parents eventually caved. "If you're not going to school, you'd better get a job, since you'll be paying room and board from now on," my mother told her. I don't think she ever did.

Rosemary worked at a small hamburger restaurant not too far from where we lived. I would stop by after school once in a while and she would ask me quietly, "Have you have anything to eat?" If I said no, she would say, "Stick around and let me see what I can do." A couple of minutes later, she would bring me a burger, or whatever else she could come up with— I never had to pay.

Despite her kindness, she was as tough as nails and talked with the speed of a jack rabbit. She never hesitated to tell you what she thought. She often threatened to "beat me up" if I didn't do what she wanted.

At home, Rosemary ran things while my mother was at work. Chuck called her "the general," and the nickname stuck. She was the one washing dishes, doing the laundry, cleaning the house, and keeping things running smoothly. Once, when I got home from school, she met me at the side door with a stern look, her hands on her hips, an apron tied around her waist and a kitchen towel in one hand. She warned me, "Don't you come in and mess up the floors with those muddy shoes or you'll find your ass back outside in a split-second."

I was careful around her, but if anyone ever harassed me at school, she would say, "You let those kids know that if they bother you again, I will be coming after them." Whatever that meant. She had a soft heart underneath her tough exterior.

One night, she violated a city curfew for 16-year-olds, and was picked up by the police. My brother took my mother to the police station to bail her out and bring her home.

Rosemary's teenage years were turbulent, to say the least. She became pregnant at seventeen; she and her boyfriend, Jim, a few years older than her, planned to get married as soon as the baby was born. But when their daughter Christine was born, he skipped town, heading to Chicago with a promise to return. He did once, but then he left again and didn't come back. He didn't have the guts to be a father.

Rosemary and Christine lived at home for a few years; she eventually married and raised a large, happy family. Her arrest as a teenager was a first in our family. But although no one had been arrested before, we did have the police at our door a few times.

My father used to go off the handle and start cussing and threatening us about something we did. My mother called the police more than once when that happened, asking them to come and calm him down. I was always startled and embarrassed to see policemen at our door, but also felt safer with them there. Most of the arguments were about money— or rather, the lack of it.

One time my father chased me around the basement furnace with a strap, threatening to kill me. "You little bastard, I'm going to kill you," he yelled.

I thought he was serious, but Frank came downstairs and declared, "You'll have to go through me before you get to him," as he stepped in front of my father.

"Get the hell out of the way, or you'll get it too," my father hollered.

I turned, ran up the stairs and outside. I snuck back into the house later when it was dark, hoping my father was already in bed. On days like that, I was thankful for my brothers' and sisters' support.

Despite all my father's faults, my mother never allowed us to us say anything bad about him. "Don't say that about your father," she would scold if we complained about what an asshole he was.

He'd cuss at us for one reason or another, and she would plead with him, "Lou, quiet down a bit and stop using that filthy language." Maybe my older brothers and sisters saw my parents when they were a young, happy, fun-loving couple. But the older my parents got, and by the time I came along, they—especially my father—rarely seemed happy anymore.

I had very few real conversations with him while growing up. He never once said "I love you" or even gave me a hug.

Occasionally, on warm summer afternoons, he would sit in the yard reading the newspaper and listening to the Detroit Tigers ballgame on the radio. I was happy to be back there and was usually busy doing something. Once, I was trying to fix the chain on my bike. He looked up at me and snapped, "That won't work!" But he didn't say why or offer to help. When I asked my mother if she knew how to fix the bike, she replied, "Ask your father. He knows about those things." So, I decided to just wait for one of my brothers to come home to help.

Maybe he was so negative because he never really realized his dreams. A few times, I heard him reflect on how much he enjoyed working at Rickenbacker and Packard when he was a young man. But those times were past. Having seven kids can dampen your dreams a bit, and I think epilepsy changed his life immensely.

One time, when I was about nine years old, he took me to a stock car race at the Michigan State Fairgrounds in Detroit. It was said to be the best dirt racetrack in Michigan in the late 40s and early 50s. After the race, we went down to the infield and he seemed to revel in it. We went over to the winning car, and he proudly pointed out its features saying things like, "Take a look at that engine", "look at the size of those tires!" "Did you notice the car has no side windows?" "Let's go look at that one over there."

He was in his element. I didn't understand much about the cars, though. I just thought they were noisy, but he was so confident and curious as we walked among them. His eyes were everywhere and I was happy to be with him. It was one of the very few moments in my childhood when I felt close to him and one of the few times, he seemed to take pride in showing me around. It was just the two of us together.

I said little that day, just nodding in agreement with whatever he said. I wondered... *Who is he?* This man was different from the ranting person I knew at home, but still, out of habit, I found myself waiting for an outburst of negativity.

It never came, and I was overjoyed.

CHAPTER 6

A t about nine years of age, I began earning some steady money on my own.

The J.L. Hudson Company was the largest department store in Detroit, and its ten-story flagship store downtown was *the* place to go for shopping, especially around the holidays. My mother had heard that they were looking for someone to deliver their weekly shopping paper throughout the neighborhood and she committed me to the job before she even asked me about it. I think she wanted the money.

I would earn two dollars a week, with the possibility of a second delivery if the store had a special sale, which would double my earnings. And since every house received a paper, the job was easier than having to learn a specific paper route.

Once a week, a bundle of about 150 papers would land on our front porch with a loud *thump*. That meant I was going to be busy, and I liked that. With all those papers, it was necessary to use my wagon, so I placed them on it and off I went.

I was sick one time, and my mother told me, "You're in no shape to deliver papers. Stay in bed; I'll take care of it." And she did, delivering them herself. She must have worried

I would lose that job if those papers weren't delivered.

I saved as much of my earnings as possible and was perpetually concerned that someone in the family would take it, as there was always an argument about money at home. More than once, my mother came to me imploring, "Eddie, I am running a little short on grocery money. Could I use your two dollars this week?" I gave it to her and hoped she wouldn't ask again next week. Having those couple of dollars gave me a sense of independence, and I told everyone at home that I had plans with my money.

One of those plans involved designing a futuristic car. I learned in school that Fisher Body, GM's auto design division, was accepting student entries into its annual student automotive model design competition. They awarded prizes for the top designs. I decided to try my luck and enter.

I saved enough money to buy a large chunk of clay—which was larger than a five-pound bag of sugar—some plaster, and various tools needed to shape clay and make a plaster mold. For the next three weeks, I was in the basement, quietly sculpting my car of the future, and told myself, *everybody at home will be impressed when they see my car.*

My clay model looked great, but little did I realize how difficult it was to make a plaster mold from a clay model and then a plaster car from the mold. My attempt at the mold repeatedly failed, coming out cracked and filled with air holes.

When I had questions, my mother's standard answer was, "Ask your father and brothers. Maybe they can help you." They, however, worked during the day and had little interest in spending time with me by the time they came home.

The deadline came and went, and disappointingly, all I had was a clay car and a broken plaster mold. My "car of the future" sat in the basement for a long time before I finally threw it away. While that didn't work out, I had more success with a yoyo.

Once a year, during the summer, the huge Mercury Theater, near where we lived, held an area yo-yo competition. I bought a couple of fixed axle wooden Duncan yo-yos, began practicing, and made the decision on my own to enter the contest. It was frightening.

About twenty of us were lined up across the stage in front of hundreds of kids in the audience, including some of my closest friends. It felt like the entire world was watching. I glanced across the stage at a couple of guys who were warming up using two yo-yos at the same time. They were incredibly good.

Seeking a little relief from the tension, I turned to the kid standing next to me, and said, "Hi." He gave me a quick "Hi" in return. He looked as nervous as I was, and that was the extent of our conversation.

For a brief moment, I thought, *What have I gotten myself into? I am going to be laughed at if I don't do well.*

The competition began when the judge called out a trick, and one by one, we took a step forward and performed some basics like walk-the-dog, reach for the moon, around the world, and others. If you couldn't do the specified trick in three tries, you were out. When it got down to ten of us left on stage, the cheering and shouting, "Go, go, go!" became intense.

With only five of us left in the competition everyone was on their feet, and the noise level was so boisterous that we could barely hear the judge. There was a low rumble of stomping feet that seemed to shake the floor.

The tricks became more difficult and then it was my turn to do the man on the flying trapeze. My insides were shaking as I stepped forward, gripped the yo yo a little tighter, and threw it across the front of my body in a breakaway motion as my other hand grabbed the string to mount the spinning yo yo on it, and then I had to turn it over again on the string a second time, doubling it, before unmounting and snapping it back into my hand still spinning. It stopped spinning halfway through the trick.

The audience moaned. I rewound it and hoping for a longer spin, threw it down to loosen the string. Pulling it back up, I was ready for my second try. The same thing happened.

On my final try, I threw the yo-yo even harder for a longer spin. It was better, but it stopped spinning just a second before I could snap it back in my hand. I was out.

I quickly walked off the stage disappointed but was relieved, proud, and happy that I decided to enter. It was an accomplishment. None of my friends dared to even try. Later at home, I excitedly bragged about it and received the usual uninterested response.

On Saturday mornings, the theater was usually packed showing a wide slate of movies for kids up to the age of 13—movies with Roy Rogers, Hopalong Cassidy, Tarzan (starring Johnny Weissmuller), Laurel and Hardy, and many others.

The Mercury had four isles, and two front fire exits next to the stage and screen, one on each side. The drape that covered the exits parted in the center and opened to a short hall leading to the exterior door, which only opened from the inside.

On a few occasions, to save ourselves from paying for a ticket, we planned it so a friend inside, sitting in the first row, would crawl to the exit, part the lower section of the curtain, sneak down the hall to the exit door and let us in. We had to be careful that the wind from the outside wouldn't blow open the curtain revealing us crawling to the front row of the seats. It got to a point where the first row, nearly empty when the show began, would soon fill up. The theater eventually got wise and seated an usher near the exits.

The morning movies ran until about 1 p.m. and then the theater was emptied for the regular features to begin at 1:30

and you needed a new ticket.

One Saturday afternoon, when I was a bit older, I wanted to see the regular features and decided to give it a try. You had to be at least thirteen to get in alone. I wasn't thirteen. My friends told me, "You can't get in."

Despite their taunting, I walked up to the ticket window, "One adult ticket please," I said, and slid my quarter under the window slot. It was all the money I had. The ticket person asked, "How old are you?"

I nervously replied, "Thirteen."

"It's 50 cents for thirteen and older."

Shocked, and without thinking, I said, "Oh, I'm not really thirteen yet." With some desperation in my voice, I pleaded, "But I'm going to be thirteen. Can I please get a ticket?"

"Sorry," he said, "you'll need fifty cents. Besides you're not thirteen. Can't do it."

Determined, maybe just to show up my friends, I said, "I promise to bring more money next time, really."

He looked at me for the longest time standing there, and as if he heard a voice from on high saying "give the kid a break," he slipped me a ticket. "Ok, kid, I'll let you in this one time. Don't worry about the other quarter and don't lie about your age next time."

I walked in, handed the ticket to the usher taking tickets. She said nothing. Standing there in the lobby, I felt like such a grown-up.

There was never a shortage of friends at the show, or in my neighborhood. There must have been at least twenty kids of all ages, shapes, and sizes on the street where I lived. There were over ten just between my house and the McIlrath's next door.

We constantly used the street and front lawns for baseball, touch football, and any other sport we wanted to play. The lawns up and down the block were well-trampled from years of abuse. Few of the neighbors on the street complained about running on their lawn—with one exception.

Directly across from where I lived was a house with the most beautiful front lawn anyone could imagine. Each blade of grass stood tall. It was trimmed so carefully that it looked like it had been done with a precision instrument rather than a lawn mower. The deep green color couldn't be any richer or greener, as it was watered three times a day. If a blade of grass turned brown, it was quickly seized and removed, and any weed attempting to invade was met with certain death. Mr. Grubb, the owner, worked on it tirelessly and stood guard day and night. He definitely didn't want us there.

When a ball happened to land on that lawn, no one dared go after it. Everyone froze with fear, looked at each other, and turned toward Mr. Grubb who was usually sitting on his front porch protecting his domain.

Annoyed—and raising his voice to be sure we all heard it—he'd say, "You kids need to be careful where those balls land." Then, he would slowly get out of his chair, walk to the edge of the lawn, tiptoe over to our ball, pick it up, and hold it.

He would stare at us for the longest time as we stood there with our hands eagerly reaching out for the ball. As if in slow motion, he would finally give it up, and the game would resume as it always did. Mr. Grubb would go back to sitting on his porch, watching.

The Grubbs had a son, Marvin, whom we rarely saw. He was driven back and forth to school every day by his father (everyone else on the street walked). Once in a while, when we were playing, we would catch a glimpse of him coming out his side door.

We would shout, "Hey Marvin! How you doing? Want to play football?"

"No, thanks," he'd say, putting his head down and hurrying back into the house, only to appear again for his usual ride to school the next morning.

During the fall, the touch football games were especially exciting. With falling leaves and a late afternoon chill, the smell of burning leaves would soon be filling the air. No one could mistake that it was football season, except maybe my friend Bill Parks.

Bill, a year and a half older than me, lived down the street and was the oldest of four kids in his family. They all attended the private Catholic school, and I considered them well-to-do because private schools cost quite a bit of money. If Bill wanted something, he could be a bully, but would back down if you stood up to him. He rarely played sports with us, and when he did, he was never fully focused on the game.

He looked at things differently than the rest of us and had an insatiable curiosity about how things worked or reacted to various tests. Bill was always fiddling around with something new he'd concocted or trying a new experiment. One time, I saw him in his backyard, down on his knees, taping together a cardboard box and asked what he was doing.

"I'm running an experiment," he said, with excitement in his voice. "I'm going to put our cat in the box, seal it, and run the car exhaust into this hole in the box and see what happens."

"What! That might kill the cat," I blurted out. "And besides, you can't start the car."

He looked up at me, his eyes opening wide. Sounding defiant he said, "Yes, I can. My parents aren't home this afternoon and I know where the car keys are. They won't even know."

Then he took a quick look around and continued taping. I stood there for a minute watching and then it dawned on me... *If someone finds out what he's doing and they see me here, they might think I'm involved.*

"I gotta go," I said, and couldn't get out of there fast enough.

The next day, curious, I saw him and asked, "What happened to your cat in that box?"

"It didn't die. It was scratching and squealing, so I let it out."

"You're lucky," I told him.

"So is the cat," he responded, laughing.

In Michigan where I grew up, the thick smell of autumn quickly gave way to the crisp, clean smell of winter when the air felt cleaner touching our skin and filling our lungs. The freezing air guaranteed there would be ice ponds to endlessly enjoy for the next few months. Although winter daylight is shorter—and the streetlights come on earlier—it never hampered my enthusiasm for winter sports like hockey (street or pond).

Once the freshly fallen snow was trampled down by passing cars, the street became a slick hardened surface for gliding pucks and screaming red-cheeked kids with hockey sticks.

The street also served as a free ride for many of us as we quickly grabbed the rear bumper of a passing car, squatted down, and were pulled along the snowy street at whatever speed the car was moving with snow blowing in our faces. Once the car began to slow, we quickly let go and ran in the opposite direction. It was a joyride.

My friends and I were not big fans of the sun during the winter, as it could possibly melt the snow and destroy our street hockey games and even backyard ice rinks.

One particular time, it had been snowing continuously since the night before, and there was an abundance of fresh snow on the ground—at least eight inches. I stood in our backyard, taking it all in with a snow shovel in my hand.

Frank came out of the house asking, "Are you going to shovel that snow off the front porch and sidewalk?"

"Yes," I said, "but first, how can I build an ice rink in the yard?"

He looked at me rather skeptically. "You'd need to

build snowbanks around the outside and run the hose to fill it with water. If it doesn't get cold enough to freeze tonight, it could turn into a mess, especially if it flows onto the driveway in front of the garage. You'd better be careful."

Determined, I piled the snow into banks and turned on the hose. While it ran, I went to shovel the porch and front sidewalk. When finished, I returned to the yard and noticed the water was eating its way through the snowbanks onto the driveway.

Uh-oh, how do I stop that?

I piled on more snow, but that just added to the mess. Finally, I decided Frank may be right and turned off the hose. The damage had been done. Everything turned into slippery, freezing slush across our dirt driveway. My father came home that evening, driving through it, and I felt his anger again.

Coming into the house, he screamed, "Who the hell made that mess in the yard?"

My mother said, "Eddie was trying to build an ice rink back there."

Right then, I happen to walk into the kitchen where he was, and he turned to me, "You and your goddamn cockeyed ideas. I'm going to break my neck out there, and then I'm going to break yours!"

I ran outside nearly crying, grabbed the snow shovel, and tried to push some of the water and forming ice off the driveway and back toward the collapsing snowbanks.

Frank came out.

"That won't do any good. He'll have to be careful walking over it in the morning, but he shouldn't have a problem backing the car out. Come on back in house. It's getting cold out here. Don't worry, he's calmed down."

Nearly every day after school when not playing in the street, and on weekends from morning to night, we played hockey on one of the large outdoor ponds a few miles from home. We rarely stopped, and if we did take a break, we warmed ourselves by the fire we'd built in a large trash can near the ice.

I can still hear the sound of the puck hitting my stick as players raced back and forth, imagining we had the moves to be more than just pond hockey players. It was fast, it was fun, and I loved it.

My hands and feet were nearly frozen from skating all day—neither my old hand-me-down skates nor mittens, used as hockey gloves, could stop the penetrating cold. When it turned dark and the fire slowly died out, it was time to go home. We'd tie our skates' laces together, drape them over our shoulders, grab our sticks, and with friends, happily head home, reliving the day.

"You were lucky on that one goal you scored on me," Jack said. He'd usually be the goal tender.

"Lucky? No way! That was all talent. I slid it under your pad. Did you see the move I made?"

"You were lucky. I won't let you do that tomorrow."

"We'll see."

Walking home on those blistering, cold nights—exhausted—with the temperature sometimes approaching zero, the snow squeaked beneath our feet and our lungs felt the air's freezing sting. Even when wearing earmuffs, we pulled our hats down a little further to cover our ears and head while we laughed and joshed each other, talking about the next day. We peered into the warmly lit houses full of activity as we passed.

When we got to my house, I walked in the side door, and basked in the house's warmth. I set my stick down, removed the skates from my shoulder, and pulled the gloves off my cold, freezing fingers. Trying to get those fingers to work, I unbuckled my boots, pulled my shoes out, and slowly unlaced and removed my shoes. My feet were numb and frozen, and the pain, like a million needles sticking in them, started as soon as my feet began to thaw out.

My mother walked in, looked at my toes, stiff and red

with blotches of white. "Oh my God! You're getting frostbite on those feet. Let's get them into some warm water right now," she gave a startled scream.

The warm water helped with the pain and circulation. As the feeling slowly returned, I looked for something to eat while planning for the next day.

How early should I leave for the pond?

Bill and my friend Jack were big Detroit Red Wings fans—as was I—and when possible, if we could scrape up any money, we tried to get standing-room-only tickets to see a game at Olympia Stadium. Sometimes we went there hoping someone might give us a free ticket. We had to take two buses to get there. Luckily, Jack's father was a Detroit bus driver, so we rode for free on his bus and he would slip us transfer tickets for other buses and the ride home.

It was a thrill to wait at the players' entrance as the team came out after the game and possibly get an autograph from one of the players like Gordie Howe, who led the Red Wings to the Stanley Cup in the early 1950s. I have a stick he autographed as well as a signed and numbered action photo of him.

Another of my friends, Bruce, was a talkative, tall, lanky guy and an excellent skater who belonged to a hockey club that skated out of the Windsor Arena in Canada, across the river from downtown Detroit.

He urged me to go with him to one of his practices. "Maybe you can go on the ice before practice and see what the coach thinks," he said.

I said "Ok", and we took a couple of buses downtown and through the tunnel under the Detroit River into Canada. Once in Windsor, the bus stop was a couple of blocks from the rink.

It was fun, but I felt embarrassed about not having all the required equipment and the skills that some of those players had. It didn't work out. I continued playing on the pond.

CHAPTER 7

After delivering the Hudson shopping papers for nearly two years, I decided to step up to something better. The older newspaper boys delivered *The Detroit News* after school and *Detroit Free Press* at night. I would sit on the front porch or watch through our living room window when they quickly rode by delivering their papers.

Hearing the paper boys yelling out, "Aye, aye! *Free Per-ress* paper!" as they moved along, trying to sell the extra papers they carried, caught my attention. If they sold those extras, they got to keep the money. I liked that and set my site on being a *Free Press* paperboy. I didn't tell anyone at home just yet, fearing someone might say, "You can't do that." I was only eleven years old and heard that to get a route, you had to be twelve. How was I going to do that? Think positive.

The *Free Press* paperboys picked up their papers in a large newspaper garage about four miles from my house and I made the decision to ride my bike over and see what was going on and what I had to do to get a paper route.

That garage was a beehive of activity and had an unmistakable smell of newsprint, with stacks of old papers sitting back in the corner and the new bundles, the large newspaper truck just dropped off, front and center. It was boisterous with loud chatter and laughter from the many paperboys who were there. It was a good place to get known. I worried that someone was going to tell me I couldn't be there though, so I was always cautious.

The station manager made all the decisions about routes. He was a gruff-sounding, slightly overweight middle-age guy who'd wave around his handful of notes as he hollered out instructions to the carriers as they sat folding their papers and stuffing them into their bags.

"Harrison, you've had a complaint that you've been throwing a customer's paper in the bushes—be careful!"

"Baker, you've got two new customers."

"Fanzone, Mr. Barnes is going on vacation for two weeks."

"Campbell, stick around a few minutes; I want to talk with you."

"Listen up, everybody! When it's raining, be sure you keep those papers dry."

The guys quickly scattered when their bags were full. I liked the busy atmosphere and often volunteered to help the station manager load up his station wagon with the papers he was dropping off elsewhere. Eventually I worked up enough courage to ask him about getting a route.

"Do you have a bike?" he asked.

"Yes," I said, proudly showing him my old bicycle.

"That's good. How old are you?"

"I'm eleven."

"Well, you're supposed to be twelve to get a route delivering papers at night."

That was disappointing, but I was determined that age would not stop me, and I continued to go there and help him out.

About a month later a route opened, and the station manager called me over and asked, "Ed, do you think you can handle a route?"

"Sure," I said.

"OK, I've got one opening up near where you live. It stretches out over a couple of miles on two streets. It's a long ride with those papers. You want it?"

"Yes. Sure. I'll take it!"

He didn't bring up my age again. Apparently, my being persistent and passionate had made an impression on him—that's something I wouldn't soon forget.

It was a medium-sized route with about 40 customers, and there was no limit to how big I could make it by knocking on doors. I remembered trying to sell those doilies door-to-door years earlier. This would be easier.

Peddling papers, I would earn about nine to ten dollars a week, not counting tips. I told everyone at home about my new job and they seemed pleased. I think my father was too, but he didn't say anything.

A real paper route made me feel part of something important. Through sheer hard work, I built my route to fifty-five customers in a matter of a few months, nearly a 33% increase in both deliveries and income—not bad for an eleven-year-old.

My bundles of papers—along with those for four other carriers—were dropped off at around 7:30 each night in front of a liquor store about a half-mile from home where we quickly folded them, stuffed our bags, and were off on our routes.

When it rained, I tediously "doored" the papers, getting off my bike, walking up, and putting the paper inside the screen door. To be consistent, I did that when it snowed too. If the door was locked, I knocked until someone answered and handed them their paper, hoping they would remember that with a tip when it was collection time. In the winter, new snow often made it impossible to ride my bike, so I walked the route carrying those heavy bags.

Saturday mornings, with a new money changer on my

belt, I enthusiastically approached each house to collect. Including tips, at Christmas, I could earn about seventeen dollars a week, and I made sure my smile was wide when collecting at that time of the year.

I had to turn in the money to the station manager weekly and some people consistently paid late and a couple even stiffed me. The manager told me, "Collect or drop that customer." Losing a customer meant less money for me, and I didn't want that, but there were a couple who had to be dropped.

On Friday nights, Cerveny Middle School held dances that I liked to attend where they continually played the song, *Perfidia,* to the point of monotony. The dances ended at 8:30, which meant I wouldn't get out on my route until nearly 9:30 p.m. To break the eerie silence of being alone late at night on those dark streets, I would sing out loud, which also helped lessen the fear of the dogs that always chased me nipping at my shoes. A few customers complained about the late deliveries, so something had to give and I reluctantly decided give up the dances.

Playing a musical instrument was something I had always wanted to do, and I decided that now since I was earning more money delivering newspapers, I could follow through on that. I mulled over several possibilities— trumpet, saxophone, clarinet, even the accordion—but settled on learning the guitar. I bought and paid for my Spanish guitar and also music lessons every week in a studio a couple of miles from home.

Practicing and learning to read music was difficult, and at home, nearly impossible. "'Every **G**ood **B**oy **D**oes **F**ine' is a good way to remember those notes," my teacher said. (EGBDF are the note positions on the treble clef in music). With a six-string guitar, I was making progress, though no one at home seemed to agree.

I practiced alone in the basement and my father banged on the floor yelling, "Cut that goddamn racket down there!"

"Crazy kid." It might be understandable if it was one of those loud electric guitars with an amplifier, but it wasn't anything like that. I was just plucking away, one note at a time on a Spanish guitar.

Rosemary would throw out the occasional cutting remark, "When are you going to learn to play that thing?" When I played for her what I had learned to that point, she said, "That doesn't sound very good. Is that all you know how to play?"

At least my mother usually had a couple of good words like, "That sounds nice."

The basement in our house was a poor environment in which to practice a musical instrument or, for that matter, study—although, no one in my family ever did either. My foray into music lessons didn't work out, and after several months, with an impossible home environment to practice, and little to no encouragement, I stopped going to lessons. I continued playing on my own when no one was at home.

The Korean War (supposedly a "police action") was raging at the time and things at home were changing. Chuck and Frank were drafted into the army. Fortunately, neither of them went to Korea—they were stationed in Iceland and Panama. My parents hung two stars in the front window at home, which was customary at the time to indicate that a family member was in the military.

After two years delivering the *Free Press*—and at nearly fourteen years old—I had to find something better to do. I would be going into high school in the fall, and felt being a paperboy was no job for a high school student.

There was a drug store two blocks from our house that I had been going into since I was five years old. At one time, it'd had a soda fountain and was a big favorite among the entire neighborhood, especially in the hot summer when sitting at the counter with a Cherry Coke or a hot fudge sundae gave temporary respite from the heat. The soda fountain was eventually removed and replaced with large glass cabinets with shelves to display their growing assortment of merchandise. The beer and liquor counters were enlarged, and the pharmacy space was expanded significantly. The drug store was a very busy place selling just about everything but groceries and clothing, and they also delivered throughout the northwest section of Detroit.

My goal was to get a job there. The store had two stock rooms, and I had heard they may be looking for someone to replace the kid who was leaving.

I made myself visible by going in the store frequently—often just to browse the magazine rack —and when the opportunity presented itself, I'd say "Hi" to the pharmacists.

One day while thumbing through a magazine, I saw Stan, the owner come out from behind the pharmacy area. I worked up the courage to approach him. "Hello," I said nervously, "My name is Ed, and I am looking for a job. If something opens in your stock room, I would like to be considered for it." Stan seemed like a man of few words and rarely came out from behind the pharmacy glass to talk with customers, let alone me.

He had seen me in the store many times and asked, "You're one of the Tar kids, right?"

"Yes," I said.

"Your mother comes in here regularly?"

"I think she does."

"How old are you?"

"I'm thirteen."

"Well, you have to be fourteen to work here. Maybe when you're a little older. Ask me then." He showed little emotion, turned to take something off a shelf, and then walked back into the pharmacy area.

That disappointed me—perhaps he could see that in my face—but I'd heard "You're not old enough" before, and it wasn't about to stop me now either. I continued going into the store every day, just in case something changed. About a month later, Stan saw me and came out from behind the pharmacy counter and called me over.

"Tar, you still interested in that stockroom job?"

I didn't hesitate. "I sure am!"

"OK, you've got the job—it pays fifty cents an hour to start. You'll be working in the back room and not at the front counters. If it works out, we'll give you a raise to sixty cents in three months. Got that?"

I was thrilled. "Yes. OK, thanks. I really appreciate it!" I couldn't wait to quit my paper route and get started in my new job. Stan never brought up my age again.

This was a real job and a bigger personal achievement than my newspaper route. I would be earning more money and even have some nights off. It took perseverance to get both jobs on my own, and despite my father's incessant gibes to the contrary, I *did* know what I was doing.

Though his gibes continued, they carried less weight as I grew older. "They don't want you there" stung every time, however, and always remained in my mind wherever I went and whatever I did.

Working at the drug store gave me a peek into what goes on behind the scenes in a retail business. The main stockroom with at least forty-fifty different beverages and literally hundreds of boxes and cases of all different-sized items had to be kept organized. I made it a point to talk with the truck drivers when they delivered and asked for their suggestions on how to rearrange the room, making it easier to track merchandise both for the store and for them. Then I went to Stan and the other manager and told them what I wanted to do. When they gave me the go ahead, I was thrilled. It meant so much to me to have my ideas accepted.

The second stockroom held a large cooler that had to be constantly stacked full. I pulled nearly forty cases of beer and soft drinks from the main stockroom and stacked them eight cases high in the cooler. Individual bottles and cans of various beers, sodas, milk, and other beverages were loaded inside the cooler's front doors for quick access.

Along the walls outside the cooler were another thirty to forty cases of various liquors, wines, and champagnes. Part of my job was also to keep the liquor cabinets behind the liquor counter filled. The third stockroom in the basement held medical supplies that McKesson and other drug companies delivered.

Stan seemed impressed with my efforts. He called me "Tario" and was not stingy with his compliments. "Good job, Tario. Keep it up!" When someone needed to find something, Stan would say, "Ask Tario. He knows where everything is—he'll get it for you," or "Ask Tario, he can do it." His positive comments made me feel like an important part of the business. I was eventually promoted to the front counter dealing directly with customers.

At home, we finally got rid of that big, round coal-burning furnace that sat in the center of our basement, replacing it with a smaller gas furnace installed in a corner.

Many of my friends had finished recreation rooms in their basements that I enjoyed when at their houses, so I decided, over the objection of nearly everyone at home, to build one in our basement now that the old furnace was gone.

My parents didn't have the money for such a project and saw no need to change the basement. I told them I would do the work and pay for everything. They were skeptical, especially my father, who as usual, questioned my abilities. I wanted to tear out the old coal bin also, which he objected to, but after some arm-twisting from my brothers, he finally agreed.

My Uncle Jim was a big help. I had actually never done anything like this before, and he came to the house occasionally to guide me through the installation of knotty pine panels over the cinderblock walls, and how best to work around plumbing and electrical issues. He was unmistakably upbeat and optimistic. If I had any doubt in my abilities, he would tell me, "You can do it." He was always asking, "How is it going?" I think Uncle Jim helped quiet my father's anxiety too. Eavesdropping, I overheard him say once to my father, "Lou, the kid knows what he's doing—it'll be fine."

I changed the lighting in the ceiling, and Chuck helped me install the large four-foot by eight-foot drywall ceiling panels. I taped and plastered the drywall seams, painted the ceiling, and then laid new tile over the entire basement floor. The basement turned into something everyone could be proud of, and it didn't cost my parents a dime.

I relished doing it, but my father couldn't utter the words, "Good job." I proudly hung the small lamp I had built back in the fifth grade back on the wall. I knew it wasn't going to "burn the damn house down," as he'd sarcastically told me back then.

The rec room became an exciting gathering place for my friends as we put a stack of 45s on the record changer and sang our way into a good time. I dug out my guitar and played along with the music.

My sisters and their friends were enjoying the rec room too, and my mother hosted a Tupperware party once down there. A couple of times when I came home, my father was actually sitting in the basement reading the paper. He had never lingered in the basement before.

I attended Cooley High—a large, three-story public high school—along with well over two thousand other students. The dark red brick buildings and expansive athletic fields took up nearly four-square city blocks and looked like a college campus in some respects. The classes had to be staggered to handle so many students. They began at eight in the morning and ended at five in the afternoon but were divided up so each student only attended classes about five actual hours each day depending on the classes you were taking.

Our sports teams were always ranked near the top in the city. I was on the swim team for a while, until two injuries derailed my participation. I damaged my ear drum when a team member collided with me in a crowded lane during practice. Another time, I injured my back attempting to do backflips off the diving board. I had to sit out and consequently miss the next few meets. My mother asked me why I wasn't swimming. When I told her about my injuries, she was furious: the school had never informed her. She stormed off to the principal, demanding answers to why she had not been notified. Eventually, I rejoined the team until the end of the semester.

Each of my classes was enjoyable in its own way, but the one that was the most fun and offered the most excitement was music and chorus. The school chorus along with the school's orchestra performed in the Christmas and spring concerts each year. I liked the idea of being on stage with everyone rehearsing together, aiming for the same end: an exciting show. The school's huge ornate auditorium's main floor and balcony were always overflowing for every performance.

We also had our share of personalities in school including Milt Pappas, the star pitcher on the school's baseball team that twice won the city championship. He was eagerly scouted and drafted by the Baltimore Orioles, becoming a major league all-star player for many years. I found him rather aloof and never saw him really engaged with the other students.

Jimmy Hoffa Jr., son of the Teamsters Union president, was in my chorus class. I'm not sure how Hoffa's singing voice was, but I was pretty sure the teacher, Mr. Aptheker, looked the other way about his absences. It was rumored that his father paid for some of the school's sports uniforms, so maybe his son received special treatment—I don't know.

In high school, when turning sixteen, my first objective was to get a driver's license. Chuck taught me how to drive in his luxurious lime-colored Lincoln Capri convertible. It was an impressively enormous car and my chest stuck out just a bit further as I drove it down the street— with the top down—and neighbors all looking at us.

Chuck, single in his mid-twenties, was earning good money working at Cadillac and could afford a car like that. Being a union factory worker, however, offered limited growth opportunities, as he would later find out when trying to support a family.

Now, with a driver's license, my dream—like most teenagers I hung around with—was to buy my own car. I had been saving as much money as possible working at the drug store.

Me and my best friend Bill went looking on the hottest street in Detroit for cars in the 1950s: Livernois Avenue. There were blocks and blocks of shiny new and used car lots on both sides of the street, tempting us to stop by. It also had many auto repair shops where my father spent time gambling away his paycheck every week placing bets on the horse races.

I had saved $325 and found a black 1950 Mercury, stick shift, two-door coupe, with wide white-wall tires, and made the decision—*that was the car for me.*

I would need my father to come with me to test drive it and co-sign for the car. That wasn't going to be easy. Awash in apprehension, I approached him. Sounding gruff and annoyed, he said, "Have someone else go and sign for you. I'm not going to do it." That hurt. He was so apathetic at times. It took a great deal of cajoling by my mother, my sister Irene and brothers, before he reluctantly agreed.

At the dealer, he remained ambivalent. He drove it, said it sounded ok, and just before signing, asked with his usual terseness, "You sure you know what the hell you're doing buying this car, kid?" Just the tone of his voice gave me pause at this important time in my young life.

"Yes," I said.

Just turning seventeen years old, I was glowing with pride, having paid for a car entirely with my own money. It was a moment of great triumph for me. I didn't realize when

I bought it, but the car was exactly like the Mercury in the iconic movie *Rebel Without A Cause,* starring James Dean and Natalie Wood.

Working extra hours, I earned enough money to have it customized, removing the hood and trunk ornaments, adding blue dot taillights, spinner hubcaps, dual mufflers for a stronger racing sound, and had it shackled and eventually lowered all around to sit closer to the ground. It was beautiful parked in front of our house, as I sat admiring it looking out the living room window. It was hard to believe I owned a car.

The Detroit road salt had caused some rust on the driver's side quarter panel though and as I was repairing and covering it with fiberglass, my father walked by and said, "Have someone who knows what the hell they're doing do that."

I told him I didn't have any more money to hire someone for that. He walked away.

A few months later, the engine developed a rod knock and had to be rebuilt. I always felt that when we had road tested the car at the dealership, my father—with all his car experience—should have been able to tell if the damn engine had a problem. Frank's friend agreed to rebuild it and gave me a much-needed discount. The rebuilt engine also gave the car a little more power and I enjoyed using it.

James Couzens Highway in Northwest Detroit was the most popular street on the west side for drag racing. I'd pull up to a red light, rev the engine, and look over at the driver next to me, who might give a slight nod acknowledging that he knew what my revving meant. The light would turn green. I'd pop the clutch, floor the accelerator, making the tires squeal. We'd race ahead until the car hit its maximum speed in first gear and shift to second: slam the clutch in and shift. Usually, the person who did that the quickest won. I could do it in about a second. If it took longer, I lost, and if it wasn't done correctly, the transmission could be damaged.

With my car running well, and Elvis singing *Hound Dog* on the radio, I'd slowly cruise through the Big-Boy drive-ins in my cherry Mercury with Bill, who was the Teen Mr. Michigan weightlifting champion.

He worked out about four times a week at a small gym near school and I sometimes went along to offer encouragement. The gym was a bit seedy with little ventilation, poor lighting, and it smelled from sweating bodies. The sounds of grunts and clanking weights hitting the floor were loud and constant. Bill, with his solid muscular body, was proud of being a weight lifter rather than strictly a body builder, who he felt were simply out for looks. To me, looking around the gym, they both looked pretty strong.

Drive-ins were ubiquitous in the 1950s, and cruising through or parking in one was the most popular thing to do. Parked, watching others cruise by with music blaring from their radios, as the short-skirted carhops brought us burgers, fries, and Cokes, was the perfect way to spend the evening.

When cruising through, Bill would roll a pack of Lucky Strikes in the sleeve of his white T-shirt and drape his enormous muscular arm out the passenger window for all to see. My hair was combed back into a ducktail with the help of some Brylcream ("A little dab'll do ya!"), and I kept the comb handy in case that ducktail needed a little touchup. I had a cigarette behind my ear and a Zippo in my pocket. Bill and I reveled in the attention.

He lived across the alley, and from the time we were little kids, we beat a path back and forth across that alley planning our next adventure together.

Friday nights, many of us often made our way to the roller rink to show off our skating abilities, and if not there, we could be found at the drive-in theater watching *Jail House Rock* or *Blackboard Jungle* with Sal Mineo and Glenn Ford. There were times when we hid a couple of friends in the trunk at the drive-in and paid for the two of us in the front seat. Once inside and the car was parked, we quickly opened the trunk to let them out. That didn't work if we had dates with us.

During those hot, humid summer afternoons with the sun beating down and a few soft white clouds passing overhead, me and my friends were usually at one of the many lakes within an hour's drive from home—Orchard Lake, Cass Lake, Lone Pine Lake. Long Lake and Homestead Lake were on our list of favorites. Lying on the warm sand soaking in the sun, with the smell of suntan lotion everywhere, laughing and enjoying it all with a group of friends, was like heaven. We had no care in the world except for having enough money to buy gas to get home.

Those were remarkable high school days, and with a car, I didn't have to sit around home listening to any long-winded, foul-mouth arguments. The turmoil at home continued as always, but now, I'd just leave.

The sibling arguments I had with my brothers and sisters had flashes of great anger but they didn't linger. There was more excitement ahead.

CHAPTER 8

It was the biggest day of my life to that point—high school graduation—and my father failed to show up for me again. Through not surprised, I was disappointed. I wanted him to see me on stage accepting my diploma because he never attended any of my school events. Only my mother and sister came to the graduation.

Graduating at the end of the January term meant no senior trip, but that wasn't going to stop us from planning our own. A few days after graduating, as the Everly Brothers were singing their smash hit, *All I Have to Do Is Dream*, three friends and I had a dream of heading West.

On a cold Detroit Friday night, we piled into my friend Paul's 57' Chevy Impala hardtop and drove non-stop to LA, arriving in Hollywood exactly 48 hours later. All in all, it was a 2,300-mile trip. We drove the entire old Route 66 that, in places, was just a rough two-lane road with a fading stripe down the middle.

Stopping for gas was like refueling at the Indianapolis 500: we filled the tank, washed the windshield, checked the tires, bought a snack, switched drivers, and off we raced. We were timing our stops, frantically trying to beat our time from the last one.

Arriving in Hollywood, we quickly got an inexpensive hotel room with two double beds near the famous Hollywood Roosevelt Hotel and the iconic Chinese Theater on Hollywood Boulevard. We were excited, taking in the usual tourist sites along Hollywood Boulevard and Sunset and Vine. We were amazed to see the new, round Capitol Records building that was about to open. We stopped at Warner Brothers Studios, and drove though Beverly Hills in search of the homes of those elusive stars. It was surreal to see all the places we had only heard about or seen in the movies and on TV. Just a couple of days earlier, we were cruising down Detroit's snow-covered streets; now, we were cruising Hollywood, looking for movie stars.

I liked LA, and a thought flashed through my mind: *I could enjoy living here one day.* It was all good, with warm weather, sunshine, sandy beaches, and those tanned California girls the Beach Boys would eventually be singing about.

When we left LA to head home, we planned to do it non-stop again, taking a different route this time through the Texas panhandle that, in places, was as flat as a sheet of ice. Driving late at night with barely any traffic on the road just west of Amarillo, we were really moving at a bit over eighty miles an hour, when we saw flashing red lights coming up behind us. We pulled over and stopped.

The sheriff's deputy got out of his car, slowly walked up to ours, and cautiously peered in the window, asking, with a Texas drawl, "Where you boys headed so fast?" Then, not waiting for an answer, he added, "May I see your driver's license?"

Paul was driving, and while digging out his license, said, "We're going back home from a trip to LA."

"Where's home?" the deputy continued, as his flashlight lit up the faces in the rear seat and then mine sitting next to Paul in the front.

"Detroit," we responded, almost in unison.

Looking at Paul, he said, "The speed at which you were going is considered reckless driving—you know that, don't you?"

"No, I didn't," Paul quickly answered, handing over his license.

The deputy studied Paul's driver's license.

"I'll hold onto this," he said, as he made another sweep of the rear seat with his flashlight. "You boys just follow me up the road a way. Got that?"

"Yes," Paul immediately responded, sounding nervous.

The deputy walked back to his patrol car.

The next thing we knew, we were standing in the living room of a small-town justice of the peace. The deputy read him the citation. We were sized up rather quickly as nothing more than four Yankee teenage boys racing through Texas near midnight.

Sounding a bit like the deputy with his own slow Texas drawl, he looked at Paul (we were standing behind him), and said, "Son, you have a choice: pay a $150 fine now and we'll reduce the speed on your ticket and call this done or go to jail for reckless driving and appear in court tomorrow morning."

Paul, looking a little shaken, said: "I-I'll pay the fine, your honor."

We breathed a sigh of relief and pooled our money. Paul handed it to the deputy, and we quickly left. Come to think of it, I'm not sure he was even given a receipt for the money.

We resumed our non-stop trip home, and that encounter with the law remained a fun topic. Mocking the sheriff—"Where you boys headed so fast?"—we burst out laughing when the radio just happened to play *Deep in the Heart of Texas.*

After settling in back home, over the next few months, I often sat in the living room just looking out the window, watching the sky change colors asking myself, *What does my future hold?*

There was no future sitting in drive-ins watching others cruise though. A couple of my friends were looking for a local job—I already had one. A couple of others were moving on to college—I admired them and kicked myself for not taking college prep courses in high school. My brother Chuck worked on the production line at the Cadillac plant and offered to help me get a job there.

"Working on the line pays well," he said.

I was tempted.

When my father heard that, he quickly jumped in with a few words that I believe changed the direction of my life.

In typical fashion, he sniped, "Kid, whatever you do, don't work in a goddamn factory." By then he had worked in one for over thirty years.

I never recalled receiving any well-intentioned advice from him. Maybe he was saving it all for just the right moment—like this one. His words were compelling, and I ruminated on them long and hard and decided a factory job was not for me.

At the time, events were unfolding everywhere. President Eisenhower broadcast on color TV for the first time. The country was in the midst of a recession. NASA was formed. The Soviets launched Sputnik 3. Castro began attacks on Havana. Five thousand marines were sent to Beirut, Lebanon, to protect the pro-Western government. There was no major war currently going on, although the North and South in a small country called Vietnam were taking swings at each other. Elvis had been inducted into the Army earlier that year as well.

I was going to be nineteen years old soon and wanted more than a dead-end job. The words of my father, "Kid, don't work in a factory," continued to echo in my mind.

After several more weeks of thinking about what he said and with no solid plans for the future—the least of which being college—I made the life-changing decision to enlist in the Army and look at the future from a new perspective. It was a shock to my family, and I don't think that's what my father had in mind when he told me not to work in a factory.

I went to the Army recruitment office in downtown Detroit, listened to what they had to say, thought about it for about five seconds, and signed up. Two weeks later at the induction center, I raised my hand swearing to ". . . defend the Constitution against all enemies, foreign and domestic." I basically signed to give my life away for at least three years. An hour later, I was on a train heading to Fort Knox, Kentucky.

There, standing in formation with a couple of hundred other guys, the Army quickly let us all know that we were now theirs. We were rushed to the barber shop, and I felt the electric shears cutting through my hair.

Guys were saying, "Ooh! Aah! There it goes," and in a matter of less than a minute, my long ducktail hair was lying on the floor.

Next, they hurried us to the quartermaster, an enormous warehouse full of towering stacks of uniforms, boots, and equipment. Off came my jeans, and on went the Army fatigues. Next, boots.

The sergeant behind the counter shouted, "What size shoe do you wear, recruit?"

"Twelve," I answered.

He pulled boots off the shelf, slammed them down on the counter, and said, "Try these."

I sat for a minute and put them on. They fit.

The next morning, we lined up for a wide range of shots. The medic asked, "Have you ever been vaccinated?"

"No."

Then, *bam!* I was vaccinated and in the next instant given shots in each arm for smallpox, tetanus, and any other disease they thought I might ever possibly contract. Crazy as it might sound, I enjoyed all the fast action: my life was rapidly changing.

For the next eight weeks, they were supposedly shaping

me and many others into "deadly fighting machines," using screaming sergeants, marches, instructions, drills, inspections, and more inspections. I think one of the prerequisites for being a drill sergeant is you must have the ability to scream constantly.

I was assigned an M1 rifle that stayed with me at all times for eight weeks. The only weapon I had ever fired before was a shotgun my buddy loaned me when we once went hunting in Michigan. Now, they had me sleeping with a rifle and taking it apart and putting it back together, blindfolded.

"This weapon is your new best friend," Sergeant Transu screamed standing in front of the platoon. "Take care of it, and when you need it the most, it will take care of you."

Sergeant Transu was our platoon leader. He was part Native American, five foot nine (but looked taller), with a full head of shining black hair, high cheek bones, sharp chin, wide shoulders and a rock-solid build. He appeared to be chiseled out of granite, moved like a gazelle, talked like a gladiator, and was every bit as tough as he looked. He accepted nothing less than a resounding and affirmative, "Yes, Sergeant!" Anything else, and we were down on the floor doing pushups—or worse, cleaning latrines on the weekend.

Once, near the end of a twenty-mile forced march—with a fifty-pound pack on my back and a rifle in my hands—we picked up the pace to double time for the last two miles. I had begun limping earlier in the march when my right foot started hurting, but now, running, I fell back a couple of steps as the pain increased dramatically.

Sergeant Transu ran up next to me, gave me a hard look, and screamed, "Tar, what the hell's wrong with you? You're a step behind. Pick up the pace. Get back in formation!"

I said, "My right foot feels injured, Sergeant."

He didn't seem to care. "Is it still attached to your leg?"

"Yes, Sergeant."

"Then you're not injured!" he bellowed. "Either pick up the pace or I'll have your sorry ass confined to the barracks, cleaning latrines until you scream for your mommy to rescue you."

I picked it up but apparently not enough to satisfy him. Back in the barracks, I sat down and took off my boots. My right sock was soaked in blood. My foot and ankle were swollen, and large, bleeding blisters had been rubbing against my boot. I showed the sergeant, expecting sympathy.

He snarled, "Can you walk?"

"Yes, Sergeant."

"OK. Walk your ass into the latrine and start cleaning."

In army basic training, there's a great deal of running around, climbing over and under things, digging holes, and playing guns, but the hand grenade range was particularly tense. Pulling the pin on a live grenade got my attention. I was apprehensive as the instructor standing next to me gave instructions.

"Remember: when you pull the pin, do not release the clip. I'll be standing right next to you, and if you fuck up, I'll be killed along with you." Handing me a grenade, he said, "OK, it's your turn." My hand felt a little sweaty as I tightly gripped it, following his every word. He said slowly, "Relax. Breathe. Hold that clip. Pull the pin. Aim at the target, throw, and duck."

I did it and heard a loud explosion. It was a rush.

"How do you feel?"

"Good!" I answered.

"OK, one more. But make sure your feet are firmly planted before you throw it—you looked a little unsure with the first one." He handed me a second grenade. Repeating the drill was no less tense.

The only thing close to the adrenaline rush of throwing a live hand grenade was crawling through the dirt on our backs and stomachs under barbed wire on a mock battlefield with live gunfire a few feet overhead. We were told to keep our heads down, but I wondered if it was real gunfire or just blanks.

My buddy in the dirt next to me said, "Ed, why don't you stand up and find out?"

I laughed and kept crawling.

There's a can-do attitude in the military that I had never experienced at home growing up. In basic training, your boyhood perishes. We heard a lot of "Work! Work!" "Try harder, you can do it!" "Go for it!" It was designed to instill discipline while accomplishing the mission at hand. It worked for me.

Following eight weeks of basic, I remained at Fort Knox for eight more weeks of advanced training in strategies and tactics. Then, I was on the move to Fort Jackson, South Carolina, a sprawling military base just outside the state capital. Columbia was a nice city with a great USO downtown and a few exceptional bars where we could hang out on the weekend hoping to score with the attractive, young ladies, while Frankie Ford's smash hit *Sea Cruise* played on the jukebox.

At Fort Jackson, I worked in S-3, a unit that develops and organizes plans for various military training operations. It got to be remarkably routine, eclipsing any indications that I was a "deadly fighting machine". If I'd wanted a monotonous job, I could have remained a civilian.

I heard that they were looking for lifeguards at the base swimming pools, so I applied immediately. Every morning for three weeks, they put us through lifeguard training at a lake on the base, but before diving in, we had to deal with the water moccasins first. As if waiting for us, we could see those moccasin heads breaking the perfectly still water.

"The water moccasins won't come near as long as you are moving," our instructor said. That kept us moving.

Once certified as a lifeguard, I was assigned to the large officers' pool that was always packed with swimmers during those humid summer days in South Carolina. One time, scanning the pool from the lifeguard stand, I noticed a big guy slowly wandering into the deep end. Then, he went too far. He began flailing his arms, frantically fighting to stay on top of the water.

"I can't swim!" he screamed. Then he went under. He came back up fighting the water, and barely managed a broken "Help!" before going under again. He was in very serious trouble. I jumped in.

In the water, he reached out and grabbed me, desperately trying to climb on my shoulders. That was not good—it pushed me down to the bottom of the pool. He let go, and I came up under him, took hold, and dragged him to the side of the pool where others helped pull him out. At that point, everything moved with lightning speed. I jumped out of the water, blew the whistle, and yelled for everyone to clear the pool while I rolled him over and began artificial respiration on his limp body, directing someone to call the base medics.

The swimmer soon coughed up water and what must have been part of his lunch. He gasped for a full breath of air. I continued artificial respiration until he opened his eyes and began breathing on his own. He was OK by the time the medics finally arrived to take care of him. Thirty minutes later, I was back on the stand as swimmers slowly reentered the pool.

A sergeant in charge of lifeguards finally showed up and asked, "Did you complete the incident report for that rescue?"

"No, I wasn't told about any paperwork during training."

"Clear the pool," he said. "You have to do it now."

I blew the whistle.

One benefit of being a lifeguard is meeting girls during the day and inviting them back for a private swim after the pool closed. I met Carol, a tall brunette, and asked her to one of the night swims. She was the good-looking daughter of our first sergeant. We hit it off, and she then invited me to dinner at her house. Not wanting to pass up a home-cooked meal, I accepted, hoping it might be the first of many, but I received orders to go overseas before things were able to get serious between us.

On a short leave back home before heading to Europe, I saw some old friends whom I hadn't seen in a year. Our paths were going in different directions. Mine was taking me to Germany through the debarkation point for GIs going to Europe, Fort Dix, New Jersey.

At Fort Dix, I made friends with Rupert from Fresno, California. His orders had him assigned to the same unit in Germany as me. Rupert was a good-looking, clean-cut guy who apparently spent a great deal of time in the gym as a body builder because he had a tight, chiseled body. He seemed rather aloof, like many body builders I had seen when I went to the gym with my friend Bill. He was married with a small child and was *not* happy about going to Germany. He was drafted and had nothing good to say about the Army.

"Screw this shit; I shouldn't be here."

"It's not bad," I told him, "Just roll with it. We're heading to Germany, and that's a new adventure. It might be fun."

"Maybe for you," he replied, "but not for me."

I had never been out of the country other than to Windsor, Canada—across the river from Detroit—when I boarded that large troop carrier along with thousands of others.

Our days on the ship were spent dodging sergeants who were looking for guys to peel potatoes in the mess hall below deck. I got snagged once to spend the afternoon working down there.

When our ship docked at Bremerhaven, West Germany, we immediately boarded a train to Kaiserslautern, about 280 miles south. Our base was a medical depot a few miles outside the city. It was actually closer to Landstuhl, a town that houses the largest American medical facility in Europe (both at that time and now).

Rupert kept up his complaints.

Throwing his duffle bag on the train, he blurted out, "I can't believe the fucking Army is now going to put us on a train."

"Rupert, take it easy. It's better than sitting in the back of a truck," I told him.

He slowly calmed down as the train rapidly moved toward Kaiserslautern.

There were over 225,000 American troops in Europe at the time, and the military needed to keep track of the health and readiness of each unit. It was the height of the Cold War, and Germany was divided: East and West.

Our squad of thirteen men was unique and the only one of its kind in Europe. We were responsible for staying in close contact with every American Army and Air Force medical facility in the theater—including West Berlin—to gather highly classified information about the medical condition of our troops: who was out of action for medical reasons, why, where, how long, and when might they be available to rejoin their units. This confidential information was forwarded to the surgeon general in Washington to help keep track of our military. We had serious responsibilities, and no one ever asked me if I knew what the hell I was doing like my father did at home.

My stay in Germany lasted two years, enough time to buy a used car from our executive officer who was returning home. It was a 1953 light blue Plymouth station wagon, not the type of car one would see me cruising through drive-ins back home in, but a car allowed me to travel throughout Europe including West Germany, France, Italy, Switzerland, and Austria.

One of my first trips while on leave was driving through the Alps heading to Italy. There were three of us on that trip.

Wally was from Tulsa, Oklahoma. He was as thin as a rail, had a heart of gold, a sense of humor, and was fun to be around. I had learned that Mike—my friend from the Irish family who lived next door to me growing up—was stationed near Frankfurt, so I called and invited him along. Mike was Wally's polar opposite. He bragged a lot, mostly about himself, but that's easy to deal with when you are far away from home and seeing an old friend.

On our way back to Germany from Italy, we drove up through France and stopped in Paris for a couple of days. The red-light district with its working girls on the street piqued our interest, and we partook late one night. Now I know what they mean when they say it's a business and a profession. Once you agreed to a price, they took you up to a room in a hotel they had previously arranged and a while later you were back down bragging to your friends about your experience. There wasn't a lot of conversation. For young GIs in Paris, it was a first-time experience worth remembering.

Rupert was having a rough time in Germany and had gotten into a serious romantic affair with an attractive German girl, Olga. One night he came back to the barracks with cuts and scratches from an altercation with her.

"What the hell happened to you?" I asked him.

"Olga and I had an argument. She attacked me," he said with anguish, standing over the sink washing blood off his arms and shoulder.

"She thought she would be joining me in the States immediately when I got home, but when I told her it could take a couple of months because I had to complete my divorce first, she went ballistic."

"What are you going to do now?"

"I'll let her cool down for a few days and then talk with her."

I watched as he cleaned up.

"What if she isn't calmed down by the time you see her

again—then what?"

"She'll have to get over it. You know, I *do* have a wife and child back in California."

I was surprised. It was the first time he had mentioned his wife in months, and with his tour of duty in Germany coming to an end soon, she seemed to be back on his mind.

I thought, *Is he ruining his marriage because of Olga?*

Other than playing on our base touch football team, after he met Olga, Rupert seemed to distance himself from the rest of us guys. He wasn't getting enough sleep, looked rundown, and seemed in constant turmoil. The clear-eyed California guy I knew when we arrived over a year ago was slowly being drained, in more ways than one.

He made frequent visits to the NCO Club on base to borrow money. The club was just a large bar—a good place for a beer and a burger on weekends. It wasn't anything like the large officer's club in Kaiserslautern that always brought in name talent to entertainment us from the States. A few of us went there from time to time and the entertainers would often say to the audience of GIs, "When you guys get home, you're invited free to any of my shows you can attend." I wasn't sure how serious they were as I was never in a town back home where they were appearing.

In one of the corner tables in our NCO Club, two soldiers from Brooklyn were running a loan shark business, and to say they were experienced at it, would be an understatement.

Near the end of each month, some of the guys ran out of money before payday and made a beeline for the club seeking a loan. The terms were simple: borrow three dollars, pay back five; borrow seven for ten or ten for fifteen and so on. Some guys never caught up on their payments.

Once, the loan sharks approached me, whispering with a distinct Brooklyn accent, "Hey, Ed, how you doin'? Need any extra cash this month?"

"No. I'm all set, thanks."

"If you need anything, just let us know. We can help you out."

"Yeah, sure. OK."

"What about your friend Rupert? We haven't seen him lately."

"He's around. He spends a lot of time with his girlfriend. He's a short-timer."

"Tell him we said 'hello'."

Then taking a quick look around the room, they added as an afterthought, "We have friends back home who collect when someone leaves without paying up." They then turned to someone else approaching.

I knew Rupert borrowed money, but wasn't sure if he paid it all back before he went home on rotation. I don't know what happened to him after he returned to California. I called many times but his phone was disconnected and letters were returned with no forwarding address

When my time came to go back home, our unit commander, Major Cooksey, a very by-the-book strict officer, who rarely smiled, called me into his office and offered to recommend me for a promotion to sergeant if I reenlisted.

"I appreciate it, sir, but no, thank you," I told him.

That turned out to be a smart decision. Little did I or anyone else know, we were about to be dragged deeper into the Vietnam War. If I had reenlisted, there was no telling where I might have ended up.

Two weeks later, he called me back into his office again and this time, in front of the entire unit, I was stunned to be awarded the Army Commendation Medal for Meritorious Service. I was just doing my job; nothing seemed meritorious about it to me. But it was humbling, all the same. I had never been honored for *anything* before.

After two years in Germany, I was excited to be going home but would miss this very special, close-knit group of men. The ship ride home was lonely. At night, lying on the deck, watching the stars as the ship swayed from side to side, I pondered the future.

Back in New York, my discharge papers were handed to me, along with some cash and a ticket for the flight home to Detroit.

I was discharged from the Army following three years of active duty and classified as a reservist for the next year. At about the same time, some 20,000 U.S. troops called "advisors" were being sent to Vietnam, and things were about to turn hot there.

My time in the Army erased many of the doubts about my abilities that had been hammered into my head growing up. But now what?

CHAPTER 9

The minute I walked into the house upon my return after being discharged from the army, I found myself feeling cautious and a bit defensive. I didn't need to be: I was warmly and enthusiastically welcomed home. The entire family was there, and we hadn't seen each other in two years. Tears of happiness were shed, smiles abounded, a few drinks were poured, and toasts were made. I received a hug from everyone, including my father who said, "Welcome back, kid." He seemed genuinely happy. I realized at that moment that he rarely called me by my name. It was always "kid".

Everyone was relaxed, and it felt good to be home. As the evening wore on, if anyone said anything negative, my mother quickly interjected with, "Let's not get into that right now."

Over the past three years, things had changed at home. Chuck married Jessie, a girl from Tennessee, who occasionally talked about her 2nd cousin Dolly Parton. Frank, still boisterous, married a girl who had been only a year ahead of me in high school. Les, a fourteen-year-old now, was ready to take on high school—it was especially good to see him. From the day he was born, Les had been special to me, and I always felt close to him.

My two sisters were still living at home, and for the first time, had their own bedrooms. Rosemary was raising her daughter Christine while seriously dating John, a guy I knew back in high school, whom she would eventually marry. He was from a traditional Italian family, and Rosemary seemed to fit right in with them. I kept thinking, *How boring all of this is.*

Meanwhile, a few of my old high school friends had found jobs and were getting married. Paul, who had made the trip to Hollywood with us after high school, was working for GM in product planning. Andy, who was stationed in Germany while I was there, opened his own hair salon. Bill, my best friend, was stationed in Korea when I was in Germany and took a job with Detroit Edison.

Some of us frequented a couple of local bars and jazz clubs around Detroit, and would run into my Uncle Jim from time to time at one particular bar. He was always friendly, buying rounds of drinks, and having a good time. The more he imbibed, the more his tongue loosened until he inevitably began telling stories about his many female conquests. My friends enjoyed hearing them, but for me, it was a bit awkward because he was still married to my aunt. Everyone liked Uncle Jim. He seemed to have an opinion and advice on anything we asked him, including various careers.

I decided to return to my old job at the drug store. Being the senior employee—other than the pharmacists—was nice, but if all I had to show for the past three years was ending up back at the drug store, something had to change. Without a plan and without a car (my parents needed money and had sold my Mercury while I was overseas), I felt hemmed in.

IBM was making frequent announcements about their latest technological advancements, and the company was on the cutting edge of innovation. Wanting to explore that further, I enrolled in an IBM-related school to learn about computer programming in the punch-card era.

Maybe my experience in the Army working with various operations will be similar to what they are teaching.

It wasn't. Attending classes four times a week to learn how to key punch cards was not for me; plus, even getting there was a hassle.

The school was in downtown Detroit and I wanted to use my sister Irene's pink and black Ford Fairlane to get there. She complained, "I'm not going to take a bus just because your class starts three hours after I leave for work—it's my car."

She had a point.

Using the money I'd saved when being discharged, and with the little I could add to it, I bought a small, white Chevrolet Corvair Monza for about fifteen hundred dollars.

The Corvair's engine was in the rear, which was controversial at the time. Some critics considered it unsafe because they felt the front of the car wouldn't protect you in a front-end collision without having the engine as a buffer. Others cited a variety of safety issues. Ralph Nader was a big-time critic who led the charge against the Corvair and other GM vehicles, eventually writing the book *Unsafe at Any Speed* in 1965. Personally, I liked that the Corvair offered something different in an American car.

At work, Stan was still the drugstore's wealthy owner, who had connections all across the city. He took his two-month vacation to Acapulco, Mexico, every winter to get away from the cold Detroit weather and spent much of the summer out on Lake Huron on his yacht.

One afternoon when it was slow in the store, we were making small talk—something we had rarely ever done when I worked there before going into the Army.

"Tareo," he began (even after my military stint away from the store, Stan continued to call me Tareo), "what are you going to do with your life? Got any plans?"

I had worked there since I was about thirteen years old, and he'd never seemed particularly interested in what I was planning to do outside of working at his store. The question was unexpected.

"I'm not quite sure yet," I said.

"Why don't you go to college?"

I had little confidence that I'd be able to get into college—let alone succeed or even pay for it. To most people, Stan's question might not mean much, but coming from someone I highly respected, his words held more weight. I knew the importance of further education and had taken the initiative in the Army to enroll in some correspondence courses through the University of Virginia. In terms of compelling me to focus on my future, his interest and question were nearly as powerful as my father's comment, "Don't work in a factory".

Then Stan added, "I know the people at the University of Detroit. I'm sure you can get in. You're just as smart as anyone there."

I was stunned because no one had ever said anything to me like that about getting into school.

"If you need any help, I can make a few calls for you."

I felt put on the spot, so I simply responded, "I have to think about it."

"Good," he said, and walked away.

The university had three campuses: two downtown and the main campus on the Northwest side of the city. U of D was much smaller than the huge state schools like Wayne State and Michigan State, but it was a highly respected private Jesuit University. Some of its alumni included the mayor of Detroit, a state supreme court judge, federal judges, basketball Hall of Fame star Dave DeBusschere, Olympic gold medalist Spencer Haywood, author Elmore Leonard, and many journalists and media members.

For the next several days, I kept asking myself, *Do I want to go to that school or somewhere else? Will they accept me? How do I pay for it?* Finally, I made another life-changing decision, *Yes, I will go for it.*

Back at work, I told Stan of my decision and that I wasn't sure what the process is or whom to contact. He jotted down a name and phone number on a piece of paper, and casually handed it to me.

"Here. Give this priest at the school a call. He's a good friend of mine and will be happy to talk with you. I'll let him know you'll be calling."

The next day I called to set an appointment, and discovered that Stan's "friend" was very high up in the admissions department. My life was about to change again.

Arriving for my appointment, he greeted me at the door of his large rustic, dark-paneled office. I was surprised by how plush his office looked. I could smell the leather. I always expected school facilities to look rather drab and cheap. This one was the opposite.

We shook hands.

"Nice to meet you. Please have a seat," the priest said, gesturing to the leather chair in front of his desk. There were two of them.

"You work at Smith's Pharmacy?"

"Yes. I have since I was a teenager, and now I'm back after being discharged from the Army a few months ago."

"I've known Stan for many years," he boasted, leaning back in his chair with his chest out.

"He's a very close friend of the school and many of the professors here."

I think Stan made some large donations to the school and the school was also a very good customer of the drugstore.

Without a lot of wasted words—other than wanting to hear all about my military experience—he walked me through the process, adding, "If you need anything, let me know. I don't think there will be any problem."

I thanked him, shook hands and left his office thinking, so *this is how it's done: have someone with influence on your side and doors will open.*

When I told my family about my intention to go to college, no one reacted much and by then I was close to the point of not giving a damn about what they said. College was not a word they used at home, so I don't imagine they cared or understood how college might affect my life.

Being a private school, the tuition at U of D was much higher than a state school. Although I would continue to work, I needed help with tuition, and applied for and received benefits under the GI Bill. It was the only way I could afford to attend college.

In the spring semester, I began college as an apprehensive night student. Going to school and working full-time was difficult. And studying? Forget it. I had never picked up that habit during high school. Growing up, we were rarely encouraged to do any schoolwork at home. When I went into the basement to study and read, I heard sarcastic comments from my brothers and sisters... even my father:

"What are you trying to do, be a brainchild?"

"Get a job."

"You're not going to learn anything by reading that book."

"He's in the basement reading... *again.*"

At first, I tried to laugh it off, but then I realized that my siblings never did homework and were merely berating what I was doing to let me know that I wasn't conforming to their way. I heard those comments so often though, that they put a great deal of doubt in my mind about going to college. And even if I went, could I really succeed? My parents were Depression parents with a house full of kids to support— they were thinking work, not school.

College was a whole new world for me. I nearly flunked out in my very first semester.

"Your grade point average is a D," the dean warned as he thumbed through my file.

"You need to pick it up to continue onto the next

semester."

I told both him and myself that if others could do this, I certainly could.

After that first meeting, the dean and I had a few more conversations.

"You need to trust me, my grades are improving," I said confidently. Before the army, I probably wouldn't have been able to say that with as much conviction and surety.

The following semester, I decided to enroll in school full-time—attending classes during the day—and move out of the house. It was no longer a good place for me, so I said good riddance to living at home. I decided to free myself from any lingering comments from those still living at home.

I rented a small room above a bar across from school.

It was old and dark with creaky, wooden floors. There was a cheap, worn-out beige throw rug next to the bed, and the walls were plastered with two-tone brown wallpaper covered in marks, possibly from other students who had stayed there. It had one small window overlooking the alley where the bar dumped their empties into the trash cans until two in the morning. A lonely lightbulb hung in the center of the room. The small bed was comfortable, and while the tiny desk was useless, at least the bathroom fixtures worked. The floor was like an amplifier every night for the noise and music from the bar below. I managed to get some sleep, but it soon became clear to me that this was only going to be temporary until I could afford someplace better. It was not an ideal place to study and that convinced me to spend more time studying in the school library.

There was a younger group of students in day school: many of the guys were preppy types belonging to fraternities. They seemed to come from well-to-do families and had done all the necessary college prep work to be there. That wasn't me. I'd had to fight strong headwinds without any encouragement to get this far, and the doubts remained.

Can I really do this?

My friend, Bill, who lived down the street growing up—and by now had stopped trying to gas cats in cardboard boxes—helped me as I struggled through algebra. He was in his final year before moving on to med school. He knew everything there was to know about college algebra and guided me through some of the subject's more difficult challenges.

Algebra was difficult, but my public speaking elective course taught by Mr. Synderwind (an appropriate name for a speech instructor) wasn't. Synderwind was a large man and a boisterous instructor. He reminded me of those old-time radio announcers who cupped their hand over their ear reading radio commercials. He called on me often to read in front of the class and suggested I consider getting involved in broadcasting.

It was in my philosophy class that I felt we were finally getting to the big issues I'd always thought college was supposed to be about. We dissected the meaning of life, studying the thoughts of some great thinkers like Aquinas, Emerson, Nietzsche, Sartre, and others. It was exciting, and I relished being exposed to such thought-provoking postulation for the first time.

Another startling first was walking into my first college English class of only about 25 students (in fact, all my college classes were small) and seeing the instructor who didn't seem much older than me. I was 23—probably the oldest in the class. At first, I thought she must be an assistant but quickly learned that that was not the case.

With a New York accent that sounded a bit aloof, she said, "Good afternoon everyone. My name is Joyce Carol Oates. I'm your instructor in this class."

Oates would become an honored and noted author of over 60 books—I was fortunate to have taken her class. She spoke softly, confidently, and without hesitation, leaving little doubt about what we would be doing.

"We'll be studying Kafka, Chekhov, and others in an exploration of existentialism. Everyone will be expected to participate." I had never read them before and doubted many other students had either.

She moved around the room and challenged us to express our opinions and conclusions about what we were reading while, of course, interjecting her own, which ultimately spurred brisk back-and-forth discussions in class. The first time she called on me, I was tongue-tied, but the next time, I was prepared and laid out my conclusions. Surprised, she agreed.

Her class encouraged fervent intellectual sparring, and we received the benefits of being in the ring together. Every minute of class was worthwhile, and what she was teaching became so crystal clear to me that I wanted to scream with joy, "I get it! I GET IT!"

I was thrilled when my papers came back with "Good thinking!" and "Insightful!" written on them. Her comments and her direct, no-nonsense teaching style were a confidence-builder for me.

"Maybe I really *can* do this college thing," I told myself.

It was during one of her classes that I was called out to report to the dean. No reason was given. My grades were improving so I was baffled as I cautiously walked to his office.

Entering, he didn't look happy and asked me to take a seat.

He took his behind his desk and after a silent pause, said, "I have some sad news." He paused again, looked down and then directly at me until our eyes met, "I just received a phone call: your mother has passed away"

It was a bit unreal hearing those words and I sat silently for a moment, stunned, absorbing what he had just told me. I had just seen her the night before when I went home to celebrate my birthday. She seemed happy and fine.

He continued talking, almost too fast. "I am very sorry.

Are you ok? Do you have a way to get home? We can help you. Would you like someone to take you home? Don't worry about missing class."

I tried to gather my thoughts.

"I'm all right. I have a car and can drive myself, thanks."

Still shocked, the strangest thought crossed my mind at that moment—I was missing my English class and felt compelled to go back and finish it. I quickly thought better of that.

There was a chill in the air that dreary overcast October afternoon when I pulled into the family home's driveway. My sister Marge was standing there with tears in her eyes waiting for me. We hugged and held each other for a moment before walking into the house.

My mother's death was devastating. She was the glue that held our family together. Her smile, positive attitude, tireless work, and unending love touched everyone, in and out of the family.

She had heart disease and died of a heart attack. Several months prior, she had suffered a massive stroke that had left her paralyzed on her right side, and she had lost some of her ability to speak. For someone who was so active and vocal, it was agonizing to see her in this condition.

My sister Rosemary assumed the heavy burden of taking her to weekly speech and physical therapy sessions. At home, she carried my mother up and down the stairs in addition to preparing most of her meals. My brother Chuck came by to help out once in a while.

My mother was a fighter. She was determined to continue trying to get her hands to work and doing the things she had done all her life, such as crocheting. Once, she wanted to show me how much progress she was making and offered to sew a button on a shirt. I said it wasn't necessary, but she insisted. She struggled with it for a long time before her head dropped and tears began to flow. Her hand just wouldn't work, and watching her was tortuous.

She'd had that stroke on a hot, humid, summer night while I was still living at home. To get an evening breeze through the screen door, she had decided to sleep on the living room sofa. I was out very late and came home to a locked screen door, so I knocked and heard movement inside. Not knowing if she was awake, I called out, "The door is locked!" and knocked harder.

My sister Irene heard it upstairs and came down, complaining about the racket at that late hour. Finding my mother on the floor, I heard her say, "Ma? Why are you on the floor? Ma, what's the matter?" Irene unlocked the door and let me in. She said, "Something is wrong with Ma. She's on the floor."

We turned the lights on and I saw her lying there with a shocked look on her face. She seemed to be trying to keep her eyes open, but she could neither move nor talk.

We immediately called our family doctor who told us, "If you have any whiskey, try to give her a taste on her lips and see if she reacts." We did. Nothing happened. He told us to keep her awake, call an ambulance, and get her to the hospital as quickly as possible. He may have said something about a stroke, but I don't recall.

I've wondered a thousand times: *Did she have a stroke when I woke her up to answer the door? Would she have been all right if I hadn't woken her? Would she have been dead in the morning if I hadn't woken Irene who came down and found her?*

There were no answers.

The funeral was very big I had never realized how far her love extended until I saw the huge crowd of friends and groups from beyond our neighborhood gathering at the funeral home to pay their last respects. Funerals take someone from us, but they also often bring together those of us who remain. In this case, it was friends, relatives, cousins, aunts, and uncles I hadn't seen or thought about in years.

My mother's favorite brother, Uncle Joe, with his big

preacher-type voice, was wailing and sobbing at the funeral home. "Rose! Rose, my sweet sister, why you? No, it can't be true!"

She was only 56.

The lengthy funeral procession plodded along to the cemetery. A steady light rain kept the windshield wipers slowly and rhythmically moving from side to side. Through the rain-streaked windows, I saw the red, flashing lights of motorcycle police racing ahead to block traffic at the next intersection. It was a sad, long, and trying day.

My father would now be alone at home with my sister and younger brother, Les.

Do I move back?

Ever-conscious of my father's negative streak and putdowns—and having spent over 23 years digging myself out of that—I wasn't about to put up with that anymore.

My father and sister worked all day. My school and work schedules were more flexible and I thought it would help my brother Les if I could be around more often. I decided to move back home while continuing college.

CHAPTER 10

B ack in school, I finished out the semester and moved on to the next one. I needed an elective class to go along with my required courses, so I chose chorus. I enjoyed it in high school and it was a perfect place to meet more people.

The forty-person U of D Chorus had an exceptional reputation under the careful eye of its director, Don Large, who led it for many years. It performed throughout the state and regularly on Detroit's powerful radio station, WJR.

The chorus held a get-acquainted party for us chorus "newbies" the night before our first morning rehearsal. I'd never been very good at events like this, and buried deep in my mind, as always, were those words my father said years earlier: "They don't really want you there."

I was standing there casually talking with Larry—a member of the chorus—whom I had just met. He was pointing out various chorus members around the room and I had my eyes on a blond when out of nowhere, a beautiful, tall brunette with short hair walked up to where we were standing. She was wearing a white blouse and a dark skirt, loose, but tight enough to impeccably define her flawless curves. Her face glowed with a broad, bright smile, high cheekbones, and gorgeous green eyes.

With those sparkling eyes zeroing in on mine, she reached out her soft, warm hand and said enthusiastically, "Hi! I'm Pat Gainor. Welcome to the chorus—I hope you'll enjoy it here."

I froze for a moment and stumbled a bit while reciprocating the introduction, but I can't for the life of me remember anything that was said after that.

The ease with which she could just walk up to someone and introduce herself—she was so self-assured—left me speechless. It made me a bit nervous, and I wished I could master that myself someday. For the rest of the evening, she lingered in the back of my mind.

The next morning, the chorus was lining up on stage, and us new members were about to join them. Larry was there, and as I was walking on stage, he said, "Ed, there's Pat, one of the girls you met last night that you seemed interested in."

I turned and looked.

"She's involved in a bunch of things here at school, and everybody knows her around the city as a former Miss Detroit and a participant in the Miss Michigan pageant."

I thought, *She's as striking as she was last night. I have to find out more about her.* I couldn't keep my eyes off her. *Should I say hello or not?* I made my way up on stage, casually nodded, and said, "Hi."

That was it, at least for now.

Pat was usually clustered around a table in the student union every day, eating lunch with a group of students. There were a couple of familiar faces from the chorus, including her brother, who was a very bright journalism major. When I passed their table, I tried to be nonchalant, said hello, and moved on.

One day, they asked me to join them, and it felt good to be invited as I knew hardly anyone in school. Being in the group gave me the opportunity to get to know more about

Pat, who seemed very bright and curious about everything.

The group talked mainly about school, but once, they were keenly interested in a new play opening downtown that everyone was going to see. I couldn't muster the nerve to ask Pat. I was sure I'd be rejected, as she had undoubtedly already been asked by someone else. Well known around campus, she was in a top sorority, and those girls usually dated guys in fraternities—that was not good for me. I asked someone else and only found out later that my information about Pat dating fraternity guys had been incorrect. She actually felt that many of them tended to be disgusting and spent too much time getting drunk.

I didn't care much about what went on in frat houses, as most of those guys seemed spoiled and privileged to me. My take on some college students was that while they may be smart, that weren't necessarily wise.

Although classes and grades were the predominant topic of conversation during those lunchtime gatherings, I tried to keep the conversation on the lighter side. Pat told me I made her laugh always trying to change the subject. The truth was I wanted her to like me, and I wasn't confident about my own academic standing, so I tried to change the subject any time the conversation revolved solely around school. For me, exchanging ideas about our dreams after college was safer and more comfortable.

Then someone turned to me and asked, "Ed, what are you going to do after college?"

"I'm not sure," I said, "but working in the media—radio and television—would be fun."

Pat quickly jumped in with an invitation that would change the course of my life.

"Hey, the school has a great radio and TV department. You should take a look at it."

I hesitated, then she added, "I work at the TV station and know everyone there. I think you would like it. I'd be happy to show you around and introduce you. Come on over!"

She was always so positive.

"Ok, when's a good time?"

Smiling and gathering her books to leave for class, she replied, "I'll be there tomorrow about 2 o'clock. How's that?"

"Great! See you at 2 then," I said, thinking, *I do like this girl and her attitude.* She couldn't have been more gracious and encouraging, unlike some of those around me growing up.

We were soon seeing each other frequently because I got a show on the school's radio station playing music and interviewing students. She had a show too. Our interests seemed to be running parallel.

Meanwhile, the chorus was beginning rehearsals every day for its annual Christmas show. Don, concerned that the show never completely filled the hall, asked for volunteers to help promote it. No one seemed interested, so I raised my hand, going against everything I learned in the Army— "*Never* volunteer".

I formed a promotion committee with a simple goal: fill every seat. It was obvious that some of the students had never done anything like this before. They were amazed when we received free promotion time on commercial radio and TV stations across the city and we had a helicopter fly over with banners promoting the show. We hung the standard posters around campus and sent out special invitations to high-profile individuals throughout the area who we knew would promote the concert for us.

Something obviously worked; on concert night, the hall was overflowing, with more people outside wanting to get in. I took my place on stage and could see in Don's expression that he was thrilled. He was all smiles and his eyes were as wide as saucers. The show was a smash hit, and it hadn't required a genius to fill the hall, just good ideas and hard work.

On occasion, the chorus performed off campus, and the most unusual location was the state prison in Jackson, Michigan. Why the school scheduled that remains a mystery.

We arrived by bus and a guard came aboard. He walked the center aisle, looked us over, and said in a strong, authoritative voice, as if giving orders to inmates, "Welcome to the Jackson, Michigan State Prison."

It was a haunting environment as we apprehensively filed into the large gray dining hall full of inmates in prison jumpsuits. Most were standing. A small stage was already set up. The warden introduced our group, and we performed for 45 minutes. Pat was the only female to sing solo. She stepped forward to take center stage and sang *I Enjoy Being a Girl.* Yes, there was a catcall or two, but those were quickly silenced by other inmates.

The show went extremely well. The inmates were on their feet meeting everything we did with loud cheers and applause.

Later, on the bus ride back to campus, I told Pat how impressed I was by her poise in that situation. She said, "I was scared to death, singing in front of possible murderers, rapists, and God knows who else was peering at me."

She was irresistible, and one of the smartest people I had ever met. I finally worked up enough courage to ask her out on a date.

Picking her up and meeting her parents was more nerve-racking than throwing a grenade in Army basic training. Her father was friendly and easy to talk to, but not so much her mother. Mrs. Gainor sat motionless in a stiff-backed armchair directly across the living room from me. Her eyes and ears scanned me for, I can only assume, the slightest fault in how I looked or what I had to say. She said little.

When Pat finally came into the living room, I couldn't leave quickly enough. "Well, nice meeting you both," I said, putting my hand lightly on Pat's back, easing her toward the door.

With a busy modeling career, she seemed to know everyone in the city and always had an engrossing story to share. As Miss Jaguar in the Detroit Auto Show, her companion in the car sitting next to her was a live jaguar. She told me that while serving as Miss Detroit, she was introduced in front of 50,000 cheering fans prior to the start of a Detroit Tigers baseball game.

"That was an electrifying and surreal experience," she said.

Meanwhile, I was looking for a job at a commercial radio station in Detroit and was fortunate to be hired at WCAR-AM, a powerful, 50,000-watt, middle-of-the-road all-music station that led in ratings with its popular, well-known cadre of DJs.

Working in the marketing department, I helped put together various promotional ideas. Part of my job was for me to take one of the unique 1890s Run-A-Bout cars the station owned, hang the station call letters on the side, put on my duster, hat, and goggles, and drive it to wherever the station manager was wining and dining a potential advertiser. I parked outside the restaurant, and when they came out, the manager pointed to the car as one of the unique ways the station promoted WCAR and its advertisers. I handed the client their own duster, googles, and hat, and took them for a quick spin. Those cars moved at a top speed of 20 miles an hour, and as other vehicles sped by blowing their horns, I responded with a jovial squeeze of the rubber bulb on my own horn.

Back at the station, I often peered through the window of the Studio A while the DJs worked their magic on air. They massaged the microphone with their smooth voices and maneuvered the many buttons on the large control console sitting in front of them. Their bodies moved like conductors of an orchestra to the beat of the music they were spinning on the two turntables that sat there. A third turntable was ready as a backup if needed. They often gestured for me to come in.

Later, when off the air, they shared their thoughts with me on the reasons they selected certain music and how they planned their show. "It's all about our audience demographics," they'd say. "We play what they want to hear." They had me help pull music from the music library that I thought would be right for them. I learned a great deal about live radio hanging around those DJs.

"Hanging around" was a tactic that had worked for me as far back as age eleven—getting me my paper route—and also played a role in my first teenage job at the drug store. Teddy Roosevelt is quoted as saying, "Nobody cares how much you know until they know how much you care." I cared enough to hang back, listen, and learn before charging ahead at the station.

If I wanted to get an on-air job at a radio station somewhere, I would need a demo reel to send out. The WCAR announcers offered me plenty of advice about what to include that would attract a station's interest.

I pulled news copy and commercials of a recent broadcast from the newsroom, and after work used one of the station's empty studios to rehearse for a few weeks before I finally felt ready to record my demo tape. It was strange hearing my own voice played back and I kept asking myself, *Is this really good enough?*

Finally deciding it was, I sent demo reels to radio stations in and out of the city in pursuit of my first on-air position in news or as a staff announcer at a commercial station.

A few weeks later, I received a response from WJLB-AM—a well-known Detroit station—offering me a job, which included limited on-air time.

Not sure WCAR would allow me to work for both stations at the same time, I carefully approached the station manager who said she didn't have a problem with it but I needed approval from the station owner, who occupied an office down the hall.

The owner never said much to me other than "good morning," if we happened to be on the elevator together. I walked to his office, and the door was open, so I knocked lightly as he was at his desk doing paperwork. He was a short man, about 5 feet 6 inches tall, and sitting behind a very large desk made him seem even shorter. He looked up and motioned me in. I wasted no time nervously telling him of my offer and said, "The WJLB position is at night on the weekends. It would be a big help in paying my college tuition if I could continue to work here during the day. WJLB didn't object."

He didn't agree. He was very matter-of-fact without any small talk. "You do an excellent job and are liked here, but sorry, no, I can't have an employee working at another station while still working here. You'll have to make a decision," he said.

I was disappointed as I expected a little more understanding, and maybe even an "OK". But it wasn't to be. He had a station to run and had his reasons... I guess. Two days later, I decided to accept the offer from WJLB. I would be working the overnight shift Fridays, Saturdays, and Sundays, reading news headlines, station breaks, and changing pre-recorded music reels every hour and running the control room board on live broadcasts.

The station was located right in the heart of downtown Detroit on the 32nd floor of the Maccabees Building in Grand Circus Park.

On Saturday and Sunday mornings, the station was the center of action and excitement as the studios were jammed with live performers of everything from ethnic music to R&B and gospel. The energy seemed to make the floors shake 32 stories up.

For decades, 'Frantic Ernie Duran' was the quintessential rock 'n' roll and R&B king of Detroit radio. His energy was unsurpassed, and he could speak faster and with more rhymes in one minute than a poet could write in sixty. His words flowed and the music played, much to the delight of his listening audience.

It was a real treat to see the performers he brought in each week. I sat at the console in the control room that adjoined the studio, and he always made my day when he looked at me through the glass with his big smile, and said, "Ed, how ya' doin'? I'm ready for a rockin' show this morning, so let's get it rolling!"

I pushed the button, the 'On Air' light lit up, and his theme began.

From 11 p.m. until 6 in the morning, I was the only one in the station. One morning at about 2:30, I noticed smoke coming from the hall elevators. Then, it crept under the lobby doors, filling the foyer.

I thought, *Oh my god! The building is on fire, and here I am, 32 stories up—alone.*

As smoke continued coming in, I found the station's fire extinguisher and gas mask. I quickly put the mask on, then called the fire department.

Lifting my mask, I told the fire department operator, "I'm at WJLB Radio on the 32nd floor of the Maccabees Building. I believe the building is on fire. The station is full of smoke. I am alone up here."

"What floor?" he asked.

I repeated, "32nd."

"OK, got it. Stay there. We're on it."

Click, he hung up.

Getting off the phone, I quickly assessed my options, and that high up, I didn't have many.

Take the elevator? Not smart.

Walk down 32 flights of steps? What if they were blocked halfway down?

Sit in place, hoping for a rescue? Perhaps.

I walked around the station and saw only thick smoke. Not seeing any flames, I took a chance and decided to stay there and keep the station on the air while I waited for the fire department.

A million thoughts raced through my mind. If there was a fire below, could they get to me? What if they couldn't? Was anyone else in the building? Where was the fire? Several long minutes passed. I waited by the elevator, ready to take some alternate action, when the door opened and out poured several firemen with axes, gas masks, hoses, and fire extinguishers. To say I was relieved would be an understatement.

They said the restaurant on the first floor had caught fire and the smoke had gone up the vents and elevator shafts, filling the building. It was under control. They helped me open a couple of windows, close some vents and hung around for a while to make sure I was all right before leaving.

Still wearing my mask, I called the station manager and told him what had happened.

In a sleepy voice, he said, "Thanks for keeping us on the air."

I paused for a second feeling good about what he said, and then I noticed it was time for another station break as the music continued.

Saturday mornings after finishing my shift at the station, I drove a few miles to my other job as a Kirby vacuum salesperson—talk about a quick change of hats. Selling expensive Kirby vacuum cleaners was not a long-lived career, but the job paid a good commission on every sale, and I needed that money for college tuition, my car payment, and to go on a date once in a while. No one envisioned me as a vacuum cleaner salesperson; neither did I.

The Kirby sales manager, a short, fortyish-looking guy with a big belly, tight shirt and pants too short for his legs, exposing his white socks, took time explaining how to use the phone and what to say when lining up customers for a home demonstration.

He was a fast talker and seemed a little shady. He had a cigarette dangling from his mouth when he came into the conference room to quickly show me how to demonstrate the vacuum's many features. He demonstrated them just once and then left me on my own to perfect my demo. Lining up customers seemed to be more important to him than the actual demonstration.

He provided a list of phone numbers of potential customers and I began cold calling to set up an appointment to show them the vacuum cleaner. After just a couple of Saturdays working the phones, I had lined up my first in-home demo. It was at 7 a.m. on the southeast side of Detroit, and I lived on the northwest side, which meant I was up at 5 a.m. and still had to scramble to get across town and be there on time.

Arriving at 7 a.m., I sensed the husband wasn't interested in a Kirby vacuum and was anxious to get off to work, but his wife wanted to see it, so they agreed to let me come into their home and demonstrate it. I laid all the various attachments out on the living room carpet. I was very nervous.

The demo did *not* go well. They kept asking questions as I fumbled to get attachments to work and show them how well it supposedly picked up the dirt in the carpet. Everything had attached and worked so easily when practicing alone in the conference at the office, but it wasn't working now. *How can I sell it if I can't even get the parts on correctly?*

His wife, frustrated, still in her pajamas, slippers and robe, walked out of the room. The husband looked at me, rolled his eyes, and before I knew it, he was down on the living room floor helping me put it back together. I was so embarrassed. "I'm in sales and know how you feel," he said.

Yet again, I heard my father's voice: "Kid, you don't know what the hell you're doing."

After the vacuum was back together, the husband said

bluntly, "Now, if you can try that again—and demonstrate all the features—we'll buy it."

I was struck by the man's compassion when I messed up, something I rarely experienced before. I took a breath, and shaking a bit, muttered, "Thank you."

He called his wife back in. The entire demonstration went without a hitch: my first sale!

Two weeks later, I lined up another demo for a woman who lived in what looked like the projects on the lower east side of Detroit. The woman wasn't married and had two young children playing on the floor when I arrived. My instincts told me she couldn't afford to spend hundreds of dollars on an expensive vacuum cleaner (looking around her apartment, she sure could use one, though). My demonstration went well, and she told me she worked at Chrysler and could afford the payments. I called my manager who said to complete the paperwork, take her down payment, and leave the vacuum cleaner with her. I did. The following week, he told me to go back, pick it up, and hand her the deposit check back. She didn't have a job at Chrysler.

After more Saturday phone calls trying to line up demos, I'd had enough and decided to stop selling vacuum cleaners. My "territory" was in one of the poorest sections of the city, and it made me uncomfortable trying to sell expensive vacuum cleaners to people who obviously couldn't afford them.

Now, working only at the radio station meant Pat and I would have time to see each other more. She often had meetings with her modeling agent downtown, so we occasionally crossed paths before I went in to work. It made my day to see her: she always had a glow about her. We laughed and had fun, walking and talking about life and the future.

It was during one of our walks that we saw a small poster announcing that Detroit Parks and Recreation was auditioning talent for their annual musical on stage at Cobo Hall Plaza on the Detroit Riverfront. Thousands of people attended these plays each year.

Pat and I decided to audition and were thrilled be cast in *Paint Your Wagon*. We both did a great deal of singing and dancing, and I had a brief solo. To prepare for that, I took a couple of private singing lessons to sharpen my voice. The show wasn't going to propel us onto Broadway, but we were reveling in it and having a good time being together.

Things were getting a little more serious between us. We had been seeing each other and dating for over a year. The Beatles were singing their new smash hit, *She Loves You,* while Pat and I contemplated the future, often parked in my car, questioning the meaning of love. How do you know when you're in love? What are the signals? Does saying "I love you" really mean you're in love? We were both testing our feelings. Mine were growing stronger for her, and I suspect hers were for me, but we also had other things on our minds.

Pat wanted to explore modeling opportunities in New York, and planned to move there after graduating college. I too liked the atmosphere in New York, so we decided to go together for a quick visit. When we told her parents that we were driving to New York together, I could tell by the look in their eyes they were concerned, but we assured them we wouldn't be staying together. I got a room at the YMCA in New York, and Pat stayed at the famed Rehearsal Club for aspiring actresses and models on West 53rd.

It was a whirlwind trip, driving nearly ten hours in my small Corvair through a late winter howling snowstorm along the Ohio, Pennsylvania, and New Jersey turnpikes. We parked the car in Secaucus, New Jersey, and took a cab into Manhattan, where we stayed for three days before driving back home. Holding hands, walking along New York's busy streets in the blistery cold of winter, I could tell by looking into her wide-open eyes, how excited she was about the prospect of moving there.

The trip brought us closer together but sadly, not for long. We finished out the spring semester at school. I couldn't believe it was happening but Pat was moving to New York to embark on her modeling and acting career in June; I was headed south to further my career.

CHAPTER 11

I was hired as a reporter and on-air news anchor at WIMA Radio in Lima, Ohio, 150 miles south of Detroit. For the next few weeks, I was driving back and forth between Lima and Detroit to see Pat on weekends before she left for New York.

My job at the radio station was a tremendous learning experience about what it took to be a real journalist. "Integrity is a major ingredient in being a journalist," Walt Wilson, the news director, said. Walt was strict, honest, an excellent writer, and a terrific teacher. He was the fastest two-finger typist I had ever seen and the stories that came out of his typewriter were clean, crisp, to the point, and unbiased.

I also met an outstanding veteran newspaper reporter in Lima who was fearless. He told me once: "The lead paragraph is most important. It has to grab the reader and hold them."

It's the same for broadcast journalism, I thought. *You never get a second chance to snag your listener.*

I covered and wrote stories on everything—farmers, fire and police, the courts and city hall, local businesses, and labor unrest at the local Ford plant—jumping at the opportunity to interview our district's congressman. Disappointingly, I felt he was condescending and rather mendacious with his answers: a typical politician who, for whatever reason, the public kept reelecting. Walt agreed with me.

My father and younger brother Les came down from Detroit one Saturday for a visit. I was excited to show them around the station but remained a bit apprehensive, never quite certain when my father would slip in one of his backhanded putdowns.

I was preparing my next newscast when they arrived, so their timing was perfect for seeing me on air. I invited them into our newsroom to get a close-up look at the activity as the AP machine chattered away with the world's news. My father didn't say much, but appeared interested as he stood in front of the AP wire watching the stories come out. At home, growing up, I could always find him either reading the newspaper or glued to the radio listening to the news.

Our news studio adjoined the large studio, where we broadcast daily talk shows and that the DJs used as their studio. It made me feel proud having them sit in while I delivered the noon newscast that day.

Later, I took them to dinner at a favorite restaurant in town, where those of us who were on the air at the station were well known. When I was greeted at the door by name, my father said (in his usual mocking style), "What? Are you some kind of a bigshot? They know you by your name?"

I smiled, "No, I'm not a bigshot; they just know me from where I work."

He brought up the 'bigshot' line again when ordering, "What are you getting, Mr. Bigshot?"

I tried to laugh his comments aside but felt a closeness I had not experienced before. He may have been proud of what I was doing but he just couldn't say it to me. He and Les seemed to have enjoyed the day as they left for the ride back home to Detroit. I was happy they had come.

In New York, Pat was living at the acclaimed Rehearsal Club, a four-story brownstone residence for young aspiring actresses on West 53rd. It was very difficult to get accepted there and Pat was one of only forty women in the club. Carol Burnett was highly supportive of the club and a resident there herself once, along with other successful and noted actresses.

The Rehearsal Club, with strict rules forbidding men anywhere in the residence except the parlor, was the inspiration for Edna Ferber's Broadway play *Stage Door*, later to become a motion picture. Living at the club—and one of Pat's friends—was young actress Leigh Taylor-Young, later of *Peyton Place* fame on TV and the star of *I Love You, Alice B. Toklas!* A Rockette lived in the room next to Pat and four more Rockettes on the floor above.

Pat's career was taking hold. She was competitive, hitting the bricks every day for auditions and modeling jobs. We talked on the phone often.

"It's a tough, bustling city with stiff competition from so many beautiful models and actresses," she said. "When I leave the club for an audition clutching my portfolio, I receive encouragement from the construction crews along 53rd. They cheer me on, shouting, 'Go get 'em, beautiful. Let's see that bright smile!' They're always friendly. I'm so excited and happy to be here. Nothing bothers me, not even those noisy jackhammers."

She was also painting, taking her easel and paints to Central Park, where passers-by likewise encouraged her while she painted. That was the beginning of an additional career: her artwork would eventually be seen in galleries from Los Angeles to New York, London, Paris, Basel, Tokyo, Positano and beyond.

Bob, one of the DJs at the station, suggested, since I was talking about Pat so much, to take a few days off and go see her. He said he wouldn't mind seeing New York himself, so we decided to drive there together.

Bob was a small-town guy and I think the largest city he had ever been to was Columbus, Ohio, and going to New York was a major upgrade. I hadn't seen Pat in five months and couldn't wait to see her. She fixed Bob up with a top New York fashion model, and we all went out and had fun together for a couple of days. He bragged about it for months when we got back to Lima. I don't think he had ever been out with a model before, let alone one from New York. That trip convinced me that I had to see Pat more.

We had been dating and seeing each other three or four times a week for the past two years. Even with her in New York, we were talking on the phone that often. Her smile and voice were constantly in my head. I missed her very much and was about to make the most important decision of my life. I thought to myself, *When I see her at Christmas, I'll ask her to marry me.* We'd talked about marriage before, and she had turned the idea down a few times.

Pat was back home in Detroit visiting her parents for the holidays, and on Christmas Eve, I picked her up to go to a holiday party at my sister Irene's house. I mentioned on the way there, "Since we would not be going to Midnight Mass, maybe we should stop for a quick visit at church instead." She said, "Ok." I had more on my mind than just praying, however—although a prayer might've helped me get through what I had planned.

The large church was basically empty, with only a few people kneeling in the pews. We quietly sat in one of our own, softly holding hands. I was a bit uneasy. My mind was racing: *Is it the right time? Maybe I should wait. What will she say? What if it's "no" again? It's very quiet in here. Let's get out of here. No! Do it now!*

I reached into my pocket for the diamond ring. Nervous but steady, I turned and took her hand, looked in her eyes, mustered up the courage, and then asked, "Will you marry me?"

Before she answered, I carefully slipped the ring on her

finger.

She stared at it for what felt like an eternity. I feared she was going to say no again. Then, she looked at me with her sparkling eyes and that unforgettable smile I saw the very first time we met.

She looked down at the ring on her finger again and took another very long look, then back at me, and finally said, "Yes. Ok."

We hugged and kissed.

My proposal may not have been as romantic as candles and wine. I chose candles and the divine instead. It worked.

A tide of emotion rushed over me and I wanted to shout out to everyone in the church, "Do you know what just happened?" But I kept my cool and waited until we were at the party to make our announcement.

Pat had refused to discuss marriage so many times before that I wasn't completely confident about what would happen. I had told myself that if I received another "no," I would stop asking. Maybe the ring on her finger made the difference this time.

For the next seven months—long distance—we planned the wedding. Actually, Pat did most of the work while still living in New York. Her friends there were stunned.

"Lima, Ohio? Where's that? Are you going to be milking cows?"

Moving from a city of 7 million to a town of 50,000 was a culture shock.

When I told my father that Pat and I were getting married, he said, "Beautiful women can be trouble," and he couldn't resist a nagging comment, "I hope you know what you're doing."

All I could think of saying in the moment was, "It'll all work out." Then, I walked away. There was no "Congratulations," or "Good luck." His reaction was a disappointment and was a poignant reminder of who he was. I wasn't even sure he would come to the wedding after hearing him say to my sisters, "No, I'm not renting a goddamn tuxedo." He finally did rent one and came—we were happy about that.

We were married in a church only a few blocks from where Pat lived in Warren, Michigan. The ceremony was scheduled to start at 7:00 p.m. Unfortunately, Pat didn't pay attention to *My Fair Lady* and the song *Get Me to the Church on Time.* It was 7:00 p.m. and she hadn't arrived yet. The church was full, and I was getting a bit nervous.

Bill, my best man, and the other groomsmen were was ribbing me: "She's not coming. She backed out, sorry."

For a moment, that had crossed my mind. Apparently in the rush, however, everyone had left for the church assuming someone else was driving her. Her father raced back and picked her up.

Father Steiner, former chancellor at the University of Detroit and a friend of Pat's, married us. New York models flew in for the wedding and served as bridesmaids, including Leigh Taylor-Young, along with models from Detroit. My friends growing up were the groomsmen.

Following the ceremony, sitting in the back seat of the car holding Pat's hand, as we were being driven to the reception from the church, a quick chill ran through my entire body as I asked myself, *What have I just done?* I felt a touch of panic. There is a whole new set of responsibilities on my shoulders.

At the reception, I noticed my father sat near Fr. Steiner at the head table. Looking at him, and even with everything else going on, a thought raced through my mind: *I hope he doesn't have an epileptic seizure.*

It was good to see my uncles at the wedding. I hadn't seen them in years. Uncle Joe still had his big voice, Uncle Ed his hissing laugh, and of course, Uncle Jim's rakish eyes were wandering everywhere. My uncles all seemed as encouraging and positive as ever, though Uncle Jim, I assumed, was more interested in meeting and talking with the New York fashion models than me. I didn't blame him. In fact, I would have been disappointed in him if he weren't.

I felt a little guilty with Pat leaving New York and the opportunities it offered.

Her friends told her, "Pat, you should have stayed in New York—you and the city were meant for each other." I think she regretted leaving, even though it was her choice. She could have said "no".

We didn't have much money for an elaborate honeymoon, I was earning less than a hundred dollars a week in Lima, so we spent a few days in a small lake-front cabin in Northern Michigan and then drove to Cape Cod for a few more days before driving to Lima. Pat had only been to Lima once before, on a weekend visit. She wasn't impressed then or now.

We moved into a furnished three-room apartment in what was once a little red six-room schoolhouse that someone had converted into two rental units. Fortunately, we only lived in it for three weeks.

Just a couple of weeks prior to getting married, I accepted an offer for a news position at the ABC affiliate WZZM-TV in Grand Rapids, Michigan. It paid a great deal more and made Pat happy too. "I want to continue my career, and can't do it in Lima," she said.

Arriving in Grand Rapids, we had nothing but our clothes and a few household things we were given as wedding gifts. We quickly rented an unfurnished two-bedroom apartment this time, and for the first three weeks, slept on the floor on a mattress the station's program director had given us. We were in love and that didn't bother us— after all, our apartment was on Sweet Street, an appropriate name for newlyweds. Slowly, we began to settle into our new home and furnish the apartment.

Jack, the news director, an avid Michigan State football fan, took me under his wing since I had never anchored television news before, and he worked with me daily on the nuances of being before a live camera. Jack was a low-key remarkable teacher and mentor. I never saw him get upset as he projected confidence in the newsroom handling numerous egos, including mine.

I wrote and anchored the morning news that aired every half hour from 7 a.m. until 9 a.m. during the five-minute network breaks between the morning shows in New York. Arriving at the station at 5:30 a.m., I quickly checked and pulled the top stories off the news wires, gathered the stories from the night before, and rewrote them as needed. I called the police and fire departments for overnight activities and wrote those stories, screened the film, and put it all together into a news broadcast, repeating that process four times each morning with, hopefully, a new lead each time.

The remainder of the day, I was out of the station, gathering, and writing the breaking stories from around the city and state. The 6 p.m. news anchor—a pretty-boy type— came in at 3 p.m.

While Jack and I had been busting our asses gathering the news since early morning, the evening anchor came in with a condescending attitude, "What have you been doing all day? Is that all you've been able to come up with for me?" I don't recall him ever once going out on the street to cover a story (and doubt he even knew how to write one on his own).

Being in Grand Rapids provided me the opportunity to interview many newsmakers and high-powered people, including Michigan Governor George Romney, who was an intense, no-nonsense individual with silver hair, a sharp jaw, and piercing eyes. Years before becoming governor, he was president of American Motors and a leader in demanding seat belts in automobiles. He had his eye on running for president in 1968 but dropped that quest after the press relentlessly hammered him for claiming he was "brainwashed" by the military and the State Department regarding the war in Vietnam.

It was the late 1960s, and the country was fully engaged in Vietnam. The streets were being torn apart with civil unrest, and anti-war, anti-draft protesters were everywhere. Muhammad Ali was stripped of his title for refusing to report when drafted. The musical, *Hair,* was opening on Broadway. Elvis married Priscilla, and in our busy newsroom, we were flooded with all the striking details as they flashed across the AP and UPI wires non-stop, twenty-four hours a day, seven days a week. The world seemed to be exploding.

During these tumultuous times, I had the opportunity to meet the House minority leader in Congress, Gerald Ford, whose home district was Grand Rapids. The last time we met was when Richard Nixon came to town exploring a run for President. Ford made himself available for a short interview, as he always did when home, and I was assigned to conduct it.

Our station's studios were downtown on the ground floor of the Pantlind Hotel, the largest hotel in the city. Congressman Ford arrived, and I greeted him along with Jack. Ford looked relaxed and healthy.

Smiling, he reached out his hand, and said, "Ed, nice to see you again." That was a surprise. It felt good that he remembered my name from our brief "hello" months earlier. His handshake was firm and strong. Maybe he picked up that strength from handling all those footballs while centering the University of Michigan championship football team thirty years prior.

We took our seats under the studio lights as two glasses of water were set on the small table between us. The soundman carefully adjusted our mics. The camera moved slightly, and we were rolling. The interview ran for some twenty minutes. Congressman Ford was open to any question and answered all of them with a sense of integrity and sincerity. When finished, Jack came back in, and we made small talk for a few minutes.

As Ford departed, he commented again, "Hope to see

you tonight, Ed."

He was on his way to meet Nixon, who was giving a speech that evening to a group of civic leaders in the hotel ballroom.

I covered the speech for the station, and following it, a group of us reporters was invited to Nixon's suite upstairs for an "off the record" with both him and Ford. It was my first time in this type of setting with someone that high up the political ladder, and I was humbled to be among some highly skilled journalists there.

Nixon was a serious person who tried to be casual, and at times, appeared to me to be nervously forcing a laugh. He seemed the cautious type. It was supposed to be a low-key event, but at times I sensed some strain as the newshounds in the room slyly probed for information they could store away and potentially use in the future.

George was one of the veteran journalists there. He was a respected and crusty AP reporter, who looked like someone you might see in an old movie—the ones where reporters wore fedoras with their press pass in the brim and a cigarette behind the ear, or a pipe in the mouth, quickly jotting notes in a pad, ready to run to the nearest phone to file the story before the presses rolled. He had a weathered face, but his eyes were sparkling clear when talking news. I noticed the thick veins protruding from his tired hands that had pounded many typewriters in his day.

George didn't dance around with questions; they were direct and to the point. "If elected, what will you do about Vietnam? When? Why?"

Nixon responded, reminding us, "This is off the record."

George and the news seemed to fit together like a well-tailored, handmade suit. He was comfortable with newsmakers and free with his advice, whether solicited or not. I studied how he probed every detail, searching for the truth to make his story better.

"A real journalist," he told me once, "just reports true

facts—no personal opinions."

I never forgot that. It echoed what my boss in Lima had told me.

Less than an hour into the gathering, Nixon's assistant stepped forward. "Thank you everyone for being here. We have to call it a night. Mr. Nixon has an early morning flight," he declared.

As we began leaving the room, I glanced over at Congressman Ford and gave him a small thumbs-up.

He nodded slightly, smiled, and said, "Good seeing you, Ed."

That was the last time I talked to him. He became vice president in 1973, and a year later, president, when Nixon resigned.

There was so much news happening daily—between Black Panther meetings and the riots exploding in cities around the country, following Martin Luther king Jr's assassination. I was on the street as the police attempted to quell the disturbances. It was surreal to see the story unfold before my eyes and impossible to convey it all in thirty second clips. I was disappointed that the station didn't have extra funds to produce news specials and longer segments. I was becoming frustrated and began asking myself if it might be time to start looking elsewhere.

One day, our station manager stopped in the newsroom, "Ed, you've been invited to address the Grand Rapids Advertising Club about the state of local news. Would you like to do it?" Club attendees were the people who made most of the TV ad-buying decisions. I had no clue why they had asked me, but local news was what the ad agencies coveted and they wanted a young point of view, so I decided to accept the invitation.

There were about 150 people at the luncheon when I took the stage for my thirty-minute address. It was the only room in the city that could hold a large gathering and was where Nixon had spoken a couple of months earlier. Among other things, I told them it took too long to get filmed news stories on the air. Local stations will need eventually to step up and invest in helicopters and satellite time, for the same instant, live-on-the-scene reporting the networks deliver. We must get our cameras into the community faster where the news was happening; we were relying too much on national news and not enough on local stories.

I wasn't sure what they thought at that moment, but it seemed to me to be the wave of the future in television news.

Pat was given her own afternoon TV show at the station called *The Early Show with Pat*. She did an outstanding job interviewing experts on various topics and talking about issues of the day, but she craved more national-type interviews.

She was busy pursuing her career, often going to Chicago and Detroit for modeling jobs. Her career was moving forward when she became pregnant with our first child, and our lives were about to change. The baby was due in late January and when the due date arrived, we were out with friends at a country western bar late on a Saturday night.

Pat said, "This baby is coming tonight one way or another, and maybe a couple of beers and some peanuts will help." Apparently, they did. We got back to our apartment about 12:30, and at 2 a.m., she woke me and said, "It's time to go."

It was freezing outside in those early morning hours and the roads were icy under a light snow that was falling as we slowly made our way down a deserted I-94 freeway to Butterworth Hospital in downtown Grand Rapids. We arrived just before 3 a.m. and at 8:15 a.m., Heather was born—10 lbs. 11 oz, healthy, and beautiful. Pat and I were thrilled. I called her parents first to let them know. Rather than call my father, not wanting to hear anything negative, I called my sister Irene, knowing she would tell him and the others in the family. The station sent a camera crew to the hospital to capture our latest addition, and we aired that footage on the evening news.

Our apartment was filling up. Pat and I, never ones to sit around too long, were looking to the future. We had been in Grand Rapids for three years, and there wasn't much more opportunity for either of us there. We both wanted to move on.

I approached Jack, the news director, and told him of my intention to begin looking around for other opportunities.

Quietly, he told me he knew the news directors at stations in Chicago and Detroit, and there might be an opening at one of those in the future. "No guarantees, but I will ask around," he said.

Weeks went by, and nothing happened. Meantime, I made the decision to take some action on my own.

CHAPTER 12

I had enjoyed the action of working in news as a journalist, news anchor, and producer but had begun feeling trapped in Grand Rapids. A few days after giving my notice stating that I would be leaving, the news director told me he had finally received a response from a TV station in Detroit that "might possibly" be looking for a reporter in "a few months". I decided not to wait for that possibility. There have been times I regretted that decision, but that regret never lingered for long.

I was intrigued about writing and producing longer stories as opposed to short news segments, and decided to send my resume to a media company in Detroit that produced major films, multimedia, and stage productions for some of America's largest blue-chip corporations: General Motors, Campbell Soup, Standard Oil and others.

The Jam Handy Organization's Detroit complex sprawled over four city blocks on one of the city's most prestigious boulevards, East Grand, just down the street from GM's world headquarters. It also had offices in New York and Hollywood.

Among the largest of its kind in Detroit, Handy owned several film stages and a sound studio, boasting a staff of nearly a 150 people including writers, directors, producers, film editors, animators, cameramen, designers, and all the support needed to produce a film or live show of any size.

I didn't expect much of a response from them—as my background was in news, not stage and film—but they called and invited me in for an interview and subsequently offered me a position as a producer. It was a major shift in my purview and future career, and I was stepping into a more creative environment than just news.

Moving back to Detroit gave Pat an opportunity to further her career with more television opportunities as well. I had been away from the Motor City nearly seven of the past ten years, so it was good to see old friends including Pat's brother, now a successful reporter for the city's largest daily newspaper, *The Detroit News*.

Initially, we stayed with Pat's parents while we looked for our own apartment. It was odd living with in-laws, even if only for a month, but we focused on the positive of having a live-in babysitter. Heather was her grandfather's only grandchild, and he did what he could to spoil her. He was a big, fun-loving, 6'2" Irish guy—quick to laugh, and always optimistic. He was a self-employed painter by trade and took a great deal of pride in his work, proudly pointing out any building he'd painted that we happened to pass by.

"See that four-story building over there? I painted that one, and the wind nearly blew us off the scaffold when we were working on that water tower on top," he said. "It was a bugger to paint, but we got it done."

In his spare time, Pat's father painted some beautiful colorful murals on his basement walls. He wasn't dull in the least, and I think his creative genes rubbed off on Pat because she, too, had that painting gift. That woman could do wonders with a paint brush, a canvas, or a wall.

Pat and I scoured Oak Park—an area just north of Detroit—for an apartment, as we felt it would be the perfect neighborhood for our young family. It had well maintained apartment buildings, trimmed lawns, off-street parking, and we frequently saw kids riding their bikes and playing outdoors.

We took Heather with us when looking at apartments, as we wanted to show the landlords we were a young family, and would fit in nicely with the neighborhood. Everyone rejected us, even when we went alone. After repeatedly getting turned down and told there were no vacancies (even though rental signs outside the buildings read "Available"), one person was finally brave enough to open up and lay out what was going on. Standing in her doorway as we were asking about an apartment, she seemed embarrassed when she told us, "We only rent to Jewish people. Most people living in this neighborhood are Jewish, so you probably won't have any luck around here. I'm sorry." Pat and I looked at each other stunned.

That was the first time we ever felt discrimination together. I felt it once as a news person covering a Black Panther meeting in Grand Rapids. This latest incident with the apartment manager brought to mind a time when I was about nine years old and our neighborhood was upset because a Black family wanted to buy a house that had gone up for sale. Most everyone up and down the street was protesting, demanding the owner only sell to white people. I wasn't sure why all that fuss was needed, but my parents told me and my siblings, "Stay home. You're not going anywhere near there." They didn't either. The owners eventually decided not to sell their home, and that's the last time anyone talked about it.

After a few weeks of searching and failing to find a suitable apartment in a neighborhood we liked, Pat and I slowly began weighing the advantages of buying a home. We had been renters in Grand Rapids for over three years, but now with our baby daughter, Heather, a home sounded more appealing—if we could afford it.

"Location, location, location" is what the real estate

pros preached, and we soon found just the right house in north Royal Oak, one block from upscale Birmingham with its trendy shopping and sprawling homes.

We were short on cash for a down payment and decided to ask Pat's mother for a small loan. When it came to money, Florence's demeanor immediately changed and she didn't seem like the warm, friendly, grandmother and mother-in-law. I thought she was preparing to check our credit score as she laid out the formal loan documents for us to sign. Her terms were simple: pay her back on time and there would be no interest; interest would only be added if we were late in our payments.

We paid her back in half the agreed-upon timeframe.

Our brick three-bedroom home on that beautiful tree-lined street with its grassy neighborhood park one door away was the perfect place for Heather and her friends, summer and winter. It was also just a short distance from the commuter train to Detroit. With only one car at the time, I rode the train while Pat took the car.

The house also provided Pat a new and rather unusual canvas to demonstrate her latest creativity with a brush. Near the kitchen was a large empty wall that she frequently used to experiment with new creative techniques, colors, and images. I was surprised the first time I came home from work and saw an 8' x 12' mural covering the wall, but had to admit, it was eye-catching and quickly became a conversation piece among our friends.

Another time, returning from a trip to Spain, Pat painted a large oil where she expertly captured the brilliant colors and textures of a small Spanish village. She wanted to hang the painting, but it needed a frame. None of the local frame shop offerings felt quite right, as they just didn't create the exact antique gestalt she felt the painting deserved.

One day we were driving by some farms while taking in the beautiful changing colors of autumn, when I saw an old barn and casually said, "Wood from that collapsing barn over there might make a dramatic frame for your Spanish painting."

"Let's stop," she said.

Sitting on the side of the road with the window rolled down, Pat studied the barn.

"It sure has that antique feeling. Let's get out and take a couple of pieces. Come on, nobody will see us or even care." She seemed ready to bolt from the car.

"Whoa, I think I'd rather pull into the driveway than jump the fence."

Before we were even out of the car, a farmer saw us coming up the dirt driveway. We stopped. Standing on his porch, he hollered, "Hello. Can I help you?"

We got out of the car, and trying to be friendly, I said, "We were driving by and noticed your old barn over there. How old is it? It looks like it's been there for a while."

"Yep, it's probably a hundred years old or so; I don't know for sure. It was here when I started farming this place some forty years ago. Why do you ask?"

"I'm an artist and painted a picture that needs framing," Pat said with no hesitation, and a gleaming bright smile.

"That barn's aged and weathered wood has so much character, it would make a beautiful frame. We were wondering if there was any way we could have a couple of those boards that are falling off."

The farmer slowly stepped down from the porch, looked toward the barn, then back at us. Sounding a bit cautious, he said, "Well, I've never had anyone ask me for old barn wood before." He paused for a moment before saying, "Sure, I guess so. I don't reckon it's going to be standing much longer anyway."

We began walking to the barn. The closer we got the more convinced Pat became that the weathered wood was exactly what her painting needed. At first, we picked up a few pieces lying on the ground, but the most beautiful boards were still on the sides of the barn, held in place by a rusty nail or two. We carefully removed them, trying not to damage the old wood. Each piece we collected was about five feet long and six to eight inches wide.

The farmer was probably thinking we were some kind of crazy city folks, but he was pleasant as we left and said, "Good luck! I hope it works out for you."

We smiled, thanked him, and drove off.

That weathered 100-year-old wood was promptly built into a frame, and Pat was right—the oil painting in that antique frame dramatically captured the spirit of that small Spanish village.

It had been nearly five years since I'd lived in Detroit, and in that time, I only saw my father maybe four or five times, including the time he came for a visit in Lima. He retired from Ford a couple of years before we moved back, and he had sold the house I grew up in that he had owned for over thirty years, moving with Les into an apartment. My sisters told me that he seemed to enjoy it there, but they also confided that my father had some trouble adjusting to apartment living. After having raised seven kids in that house, he had difficulty letting it go and would frequently drive past after it had been sold.

From what I could gather—and from what my siblings said—healthwise, he was in decent shape for his age. He dealt with constant pain in his legs, his feet felt like they were asleep most of the time due to damage caused from years working in a factory, and he was supposedly still taking medicine for epilepsy.

I perpetually hoped he continued with his medication because without it, anything could happen. My mother had constantly warned, "You're going to kill yourself driving one day if you don't take your pills."

That exact tragedy struck in the afternoon of January 3, 1969. My father had been driving home from visiting my sister Irene and her husband Paul. Alone in the car, he suffered an epileptic seizure. His body stiffened with his foot on the gas pedal, and the car sped out of control and rammed into the rear of a large parked truck. The front end of the car was demolished. On impact, he lunged forward into the steering wheel, which crushed his chest. Paramedics rushed him to Mount Carmel Hospital in Northwest Detroit—ironically the same hospital my mother had been in so often with her heart condition.

Irene called me, and I rushed to the hospital. My brothers and sisters were already there standing outside the ICU where the doctors had him under heavy sedation following emergency surgery. My sister's eyes were red from crying.

The doctor couldn't be certain whether he would survive his injuries—there was internal bleeding, and he was in critical condition. Later when we were allowed to go into the room, I hesitated for a few seconds, not knowing what my reaction would be on seeing him lying in the stark ICU bed with his head and chest bandaged and tubes being fed into his arm and chest from the hanging IV bags while a monitoring screen showed a beating heart. The room had a strong antiseptic smell and the temperature was very cool, as it usually is in hospital rooms. Quickly scanning the room, I looked at my father, and found it heartbreaking because he looked so helpless, and that's not the way he ever wanted others to see him. I was saddened.

For the next couple of days, it was a wait-and-pray situation.

My father lay in the hospital for the next two days and we hoped for the best, but it wasn't to be—he suffered a pulmonary embolism, a blood clot moved to his lungs and killed him. A nurse in the room at the time said her back was to him when she heard him suddenly cough and let out a choking sound. When she turned around, he was gone.

It was Sunday, January 5.

Chuck called, "Hello. Eddie?"

"Yes."

I could hear the pain in his voice when he uttered the words, "Daddy died." I heard a sniffle, a clearing of the throat, a swallow, and his voice broke.

Trying to regain composure, Chuck said, "They couldn't do much for him."

Louis Tar's death was broadcast on the radio as Detroit's first traffic-related fatality of 1969. Not a story or statistic one wants to hear. He was 67.

It was especially poignant that he died as my mother often warned him he would—from injuries in an auto accident that was caused by an epileptic seizure.

The funeral home was all too familiar—it was the same one where my mother had been laid out just a little over six years earlier. Nothing had changed, including the funeral director. Funeral homes, even empty, are creepy places with a dull smell about them, and in the winter even more so as the doors are always closed tight.

I was surprised my older brothers and sisters who were so close to my father didn't have anyone in mind, a priest or minister, to come to the funeral home to deliver a short eulogy. They got into a ridiculous debate that since he wasn't Catholic, they couldn't ask a priest. I thought, *Why not?* No one was able to come up with a minister, so I stepped forward and suggested Father Steiner, who married Pat and me. He'd sat near my father at the head table during our wedding reception three and a half years ago, so maybe they had become acquainted.

Father Steiner was a good friend of Pat's, and I asked her to contact him to see if he would deliver a short eulogy. He was more than gracious, and readily agreed. He had always been encouraging and open to helping Pat in any way he could.

Father Steiner was short, slight in build, had thinning hair, spoke softly, but was not shy. He offered his opinion on anything and everything. Once, Pat asked if he was ever shocked or surprised to hear about scandals in the church.

He replied, "I wouldn't be surprised if the pope himself walked in with a girl on each arm."

At the funeral home, he was urbane, and sensitive to the family. Father Steiner delivered a short eulogy commenting at one point, "I only met Louis Tar once, but from what I've seen of his seven children—and many grandchildren and friends in this room—he was loved and must have been a terrific father, grandfather, and friend."

We appreciated his kind words, though I couldn't help but think: *What would he have thought if he knew the same "Lou" I did growing up.* My father's inability to be positive always hurt, and his constant barrage of disparaging words will remain burned in my mind forever. It was sad that we never had any close conversations as he seemed to have with my older brothers and sisters, and now we never would.

Pat and I drove Father Steiner back to the University and thanked him. My brother Les—just shy of 22 years old, with long hair, and a motorcycle—was now alone in the apartment. He was concerned more about the draft lottery than anything else. Attending junior college, Les was hoping for a college deferment or simply not getting a high number in the lottery. I told him going to college part-time may not be enough for a deferment and encouraged him to attend full-time. He didn't, but luckily, his number never came up.

Pat maintained her "anything is possible" attitude. In addition to taking care of Heather and building a home, her modeling career was moving along, and as a result, she was flying to New York for various jobs. It was always a surprise to see what out of the ordinary shopping finds she would come home with, and I was amazed that she even found time to do any shopping there at all.

How she convinced the airline to allow her to check two unwrapped 30-inch-long Spanish swords she had bought at a New York antique shop is beyond me, but she did. Another time, she carried on board a beautiful one-of-a-kind antique, hand-carved solid-wood Aboriginal stool. The flight attendant simply placed it in the plane cabin's closet—I couldn't believe it.

The stool went perfectly in our home, as did the swords hanging over the fireplace with Pat's Spanish painting in its antique frame hanging on the wall near them. It all looked good to me, but Pat had other ideas. She walked around the room studying the walls from every angle, running her hands across their smooth surfaces.

Ever the creative artist, she said, "We need to change the wall above and on both sides of the fireplace."

"What color do you want to paint them?" I asked.

"I want to do more than paint them. How about something more rustic?"

From time to time, my warning light went on, and this was one of those times. Trying to not appear concerned, "Rustic? What did you have in mind?"

"How about putting some straw on the walls?"

With a slight bit of panic in my voice, I blurted, "Straw? On the walls? That's ridiculous. We can't just add straw; we would have to completely replaster them. They would look terrible."

"I think they'll look terrific. It'll pick up the entire room—you know how to do that."

Pat was always encouraging about my ability to do something, even when I didn't have any clue how to do it. Now growing more serious (since she clearly sounded convinced of what she wanted to do), I said, "It would be easier to move those things than replaster the walls."

She came over to me, gave me a kiss on the cheek, and smiled, "Come on, honey. It'll be fun, and I will help in any way you want. If we don't like it, we can change it back."

That was Pat: anything is possible.

I thought, *there's no going back once we start.*

Before I knew it, we had a small bundle of hay, plaster, and every tool necessary. Pat turned into a supervisor. After finishing, I had to admit those walls looked good—and quite rustic with that straw coming through the rough plaster. The swords looked dramatic, crisscrossed above the fireplace, and the walls were perfect for her paintings. Some of our friends were shocked that we would "destroy" our walls like that.

We laughed. "We didn't destroy them, we improved them," she said.

An imaginative, can-do attitude worked wonders at home. At work, on the other hand, my way of thinking and questioning why something had to be done a certain way caused me some real headaches.

CHAPTER 13

Working in mid-town Detroit on East Grand Blvd was a commuting headache. We only had one car, and since Pat needed to get to her auditions, I became a train commuter for the first time in my life. I had no particular desire to be one and wasn't a big fan of the train. After several months of doing that, Pat and I looked at each other, and almost in unison, said, "We need a second car!" We had spent too much time trying to make one car work for two active people.

I had my sights set on something small and sporty— maybe a used two-seat MG or something similar—but Pat had other ideas. She saw a "For Sale by Owner" ad for a Porsche in the newspaper. I figured she would soon realize that something other than a Porsche would be a better value and more affordable, so I agreed to "at least take a look at it". That was a mistake.

We saw it, drove it, and talked at length with the owner. The more we talked, the more he whittled the price down until we reached an agreement. We were now the owners of a red 1968 Porsche 912. We loved the car. Pat immediately claimed exclusive use, and with the Porsche's stick shift and racing image, it fit her perfectly. Our best friends Cheryl and

Bill also had a Porsche, and that made for a lot of friendly conversations between car lovers.

Our car nearly went totally up in flames while pumping gas one time at a gas station. Smoke began bellowing out of the engine compartment and then there was a fire. Luckily, the fire was not near the gas tank, and a quick-acting attendant with a fire extinguisher put it out. I wanted to sell the car after that incident, but we had it repaired instead. The red Porsche was part of the family and remained with us for years until Pat sustained some serious injuries when she was rear-ended by a large, full-sized Ford on the freeway. Our Porsche came out severely damaged and it was too costly to repair.

Working in Detroit, and becoming accustomed to a slower pace than the news business, was a challenge. I was used to deadlines defined by seconds, not days. In television news, our goal was to get the facts quickly and accurately. We then finished the story, aired it, and charged on to the next one.

My new job entailed dealing with people and companies who didn't seem to possess the sense of urgency in the same way that I was accustomed to. Writing a script, shooting, and editing a film shouldn't be complicated, but when it's done in a committee-type atmosphere, the process can be very slow. There were often six or seven rewrites and layers of people involved in the final approval process, many of whom had their own agendas.

This slow pacing got me into hot water more than once. When I was assigned to produce a film for an auto company, I thought the crew was too large and would slow production, so I suggested reducing its size, but the VP of production wasn't on board. "I don't care how large the crew is, just go along with what the director wants. GM is paying for it, and it's near the end of their fiscal year—if they have money left in the budget and don't spend it, their budget will be cut next year," he said. I thought, *What a sorry way to do business.*

Another time, I was producing a large live stage event at the Doral Hotel in Miami, Florida. When it ended, the union steward for the stagehands—an older gentleman who looked like he had been in the union a few too many years—came up to me with the labor timesheets to sign. Timesheets detail how much union labor was used, including start times, end times, and overtime. As I reviewed them, I noticed that the work times and overtime listed were not in agreement with my notes on the time worked. I pointed it out and asked him to please correct it. Standing there with him backstage, he became very uneasy and defensive, and said, "I'm not doing that. They are correct and need to be signed."

To me, the time sheets looked padded. Apparently, no one had ever questioned him before. Looking a little upset (to say the least), he warned, "If you're not going to sign these, I will report it back to your company."

We were in a standoff as I wasn't about to sign them.

I got to the office the next day and was immediately called into the VP of production's office. He was a middle-aged man, who always seem to wear shirts that were too tight exposing a rather large belly, and his tie likewise seemed to be perpetually too tight; he came to work each day at 9 a.m. and tried to be gone at 5 p.m. He didn't want to make waves, and his backbone was nonexistent.

I explained that the union was padding the timesheet and requested it be corrected. The production chief, raising his voice and turning a little red, said, "You must sign these sheets. I don't want any union problems. I can make the corrections, if any are needed."

"OK," I said, and left the office thinking he wouldn't stand up to the union even if his life depended on it. This wouldn't be the last time I questioned how things were done.

Woodstock had passed, and as the 70s unfolded, there was new management coming into our company. The new CEO asked some of the same questions I had. Why are we doing things a certain way? Can't it be done better and cheaper? Who is responsible?

I was assigned to produce a film for a new client from the West Coast, Toyota. Our film department laid out a scenario where we would fly a film crew from Detroit to Los Angeles for the project. Finding that ridiculous, I proposed using a local Hollywood crew to save money.

"Just because it's in the budget doesn't mean we need a full crew of nearly twenty people," I said. "I can do it with half the people and still deliver a top-quality film on time and for less money."

This was not a popular position, as I was again questioning their long-held way of doing things. The manager remained skeptical of what I wanted to do, and it reminded me of when my father had so often said to me, "Do you know what the hell you're doing, kid?"

After providing him with more details about how I intended to handle the filming, I was finally given the go-ahead, and it put me on the spot.

A year earlier, a staff director/cameraman who had worked with our company had moved to Hollywood to work his way into feature films, so I quickly contacted him and outlined my idea of filming with a smaller crew, and the freedom to set our own creative path. Lee would be given control of the creative aspect and how and where to film. At first, he was reluctant, but as we talked, he slowly started to come around. He liked the freedom of creative control.

I flew to Hollywood and we mapped it out together, selecting locations that were free of costly fees and permits. Our crew was paid flat fees—which included any overtime—our on-camera talent was hired locally, up in Lake Arrowhead, where we were filming, and we didn't use any talent agents. I had worked out special deals for all our equipment rentals. We finished the filming on time, under budget, and it looked beautiful. Everyone was pleased, including the client.

While in California, I took a day to visit my sister Irene and her husband, who had moved there the previous year. They had a beautiful home high up in the hills overlooking the San Fernando Valley, and that subliminal longing to live in California quickly flashed through my mind again.

At work, I continued to push that there were often better ways of doing things rather than just accepting, "that's the way it's always been done."

I was given the assignment to capture on film the excitement of the day-to-day action at Hamburger U, the McDonald's Training facility near Chicago, and incorporate the photography into a larger film we were producing. Sounds simple enough and I made the decision to hire a photographer we had not used before who I met through a designer friend. Tom Bert was a long-haired, hippie-type cameraman at the time, whose specialty was photographing people and celebrities. "I need people in action," I told him, "Not staged photography."

He was cautious, as he didn't typically shoot much corporate or "stiff photography", as he called it. We agreed that he would shoot nearly everything loose, dynamic, and handheld, leveraging various angles and a variety of light sources. We spent two days at Hamburger U, surrounded by the smell of hamburgers and French fries, capturing the excitement and fast-moving action going on during training. Tom's creative photography captured the emotion of people in action. It was exciting to see.

When I got back to the office, our creative director on the account questioned everything, picking apart infinite details, and finally summing it up with, "The client is not going to be happy with this."

"Look, let's just present it—it's real," I responded. We did and they loved it.

It's amazing to me that people in business are often afraid to step out and try something different. Tom and I did, and it worked.

He eventually moved to Hollywood and became a leading photographer in tinseltown. We've had a few laughs now and again, reminiscing about how exposed and alone we felt going against the grain, but clearly, it was worth the anxiety for both of us.

Plodding along as a staff producer was getting rather routine when our company was sold to a New York studio, Teletape. That excited me because I understood the television studio business.

On one of my trips to New York, the studio manager gave me the twenty-five cent "cook's tour". In the early days of Sesame Street, Children's Television Workshop rented one of our stages there, so I thought it would be fun to take a feather from Big Bird's costume home to our then four-year-old daughter, Heather, back in Detroit. I still have the feather. It was a big deal, as Sesame Street was so new at the time and no kid could say they had a real feather from Big Bird.

During my four years working at Jam Handy—now Teletape—many things were changing and I still had some unfinished business, namely, a college degree.

College had been interrupted during my journalism career in Lima and Grand Rapids, and with our growing family, it was difficult to accomplish everything at one time. I enrolled back at the University of Detroit, and this time, it was much simpler than it had been years earlier. I sailed through my final courses with very high marks and received my B.A. degree, with minors in English and philosophy.

All those years doubting my ability to succeed in college and the hundreds of times I had asked myself, "Can I really do this?" were all finally answered. Despite the utter lack of support in academia growing up, I had done it! I am now a college graduate, the only one in my entire family of seven kids.

Participating in my college graduation ceremonies, hearing my name called, and walking up on stage to accept my diploma was truly special with Pat and Heather there celebrating alongside me. I was proud of graduating and thought *just maybe* my father might have been proud of me too. He probably wouldn't have attended the ceremony—or even acknowledged my accomplishment—but deep down, I like to think he might have, just this one time. The future looked bright, through the lenses of a man who hadn't given up on college.

Pat and I had erased the words "giving up" from our vocabulary in everything we did, whether professionally or just in enjoying each other's company.

Once, we were going out for a fun weekend of snowmobiling at a friend's home out in the country about 75 miles north of Detroit. It was the dead of winter, and snow began falling on Friday morning, as forecast. Since we were planning on leaving in the early afternoon, we expected to be there by the time any heavy snow fell. Unfortunately, we left later than planned and had to drop Heather off with Pat's brother Paul, who was babysitting for the weekend. It was dark by the time we filled up with gas and began heading north on the highway.

The gas station attendant warned us, "Driving conditions are bad; even truckers aren't moving."

Determined, we took off on what would normally be a little over an hour's drive. The snow and wind soon picked up, and the blizzard-like conditions soon forced me to slow to about fifteen miles an hour. The snow was getting deeper, and snowplows were nonexistent. That gas station attendant was right: there was not a single truck on the road. The radio likewise encouraged people to stay indoors, but it was too late for us—turning back would be just as hazardous as plodding ahead to our destination.

I wasn't feeling good about our situation, but at least the gas tank was full if we needed to run the engine for warmth should we need to pull over or God forbid, spend the night in the car. We had plenty of warm clothes with us, so that offered some additional comfort.

Finally, when I couldn't see the highway any longer and the snow was just too deep to continue, I pulled over and stopped. We had been sitting there for a while wondering what to do when we heard a knock on the window. Standing there was a guy covered from head to toe in snow gear with only his eyes showing. I rolled the window down a bit.

Yelling through his face mask behind the howling wind, he asked in a husky, deep-throated whiskey voice, "You folks need any help?"

"Yes," I said. "We're heading to this place." I slipped him a piece of paper containing our friend's address through the partially opened window. "We're not sure where the highway exit is."

He shined his flashlight on the blowing paper and turned to us, and said, "The exits are all closed ahead, but where you're going isn't very far—I know where it is. You're not going to be moving on the roads in this storm. You can leave your car here, if you want; I can take one of you there on my snowmobile and come back for the other one."

I looked at Pat and she at me.

Pausing, I said, "Ok, take her."

Pat looked at me in shock and whispered, "We don't know who this guy is, and I'm supposed to go alone with him?"

We stared at each other for a moment.

Sensing our hesitation, the gentleman said, "The snow is getting worse, and we'll all be snowed in before it ends."

"How far is it?" I asked.

"Just up the road a bit."

"OK," I said and nudged Pat a little.

She gave me another razor-sharp look, reluctantly grabbed her small bag, and couldn't resist piercing me with her eyes one last time as she got out of the car. Pat hopped on the back of his snowmobile, and away they went. In a couple of seconds, they were out of sight, and then it struck me, *Am I crazy? I just let my wife get on a snowmobile with a guy, who for all I know, is the next Boston Strangler.*

All sorts of thoughts raced through my mind as I sat alone in the car waiting for him to return: *What if he just kidnapped her? What if he doesn't return? I don't have a clue where I am.* The windows began fogging up, and I started the car to defrost them and get some heat.

After what seemed like an eternity (but was in fact probably only twenty-five minutes or so), I heard a knock on the window. It was him.

"I got her there. It's your turn," he said. "Hop on."

Relieved, I grabbed my small bag, got out, locked the car and "hopped on". Locking the car was a habit, but also laughable—no one was out stealing cars in this storm.

Racing through the dark, I could see the snow blowing horizontally in the beam of our headlight. The stinging, freezing wind felt like it was peeling the skin off my face, and I couldn't stop wondering, *Is Pat Ok? Who is this guy?* We couldn't hear each other over the raging wind and the snowmobile's engine, so I had to trust him. In a few minutes, we pulled up to a home.

"Here's where I dropped off your wife," he hollered.

I was getting off the snowmobile when the house doors burst open. Pat and our friends were smiling, cheering, and shouting for me to come in out of the cold and snow. I took my first relaxed breath in quite a while.

The snowmobile driver apparently owned a home somewhere in the area. He told us he always kept an eye on the road for stranded motorists during this kind of weather. We invited him in.

"No, thanks," he said. "I'm going to be heading back to the highway one last time. This is the worst storm I've seen in quite a while."

Just as quickly as he had appeared, he vanished, and I almost felt he gave a wink and a nod as if heading back up the chimney. We never saw him again and wonder if he is still out there, "heading back to the highway" whenever it snows.

Our friends had all but given up on us, but Cheryl, Pat's best friend, said happily, "If there's a way, I know Pat would never let a little snow stop her."

I thought, *"A little snow? There must be a couple of feet on the road!*

The snow continued throughout Saturday as we enjoyed snowmobiling. Sunday afternoon, we made it back to the highway, now cleared by snowplows. On the side of the road, right where we had left it, our car sat smiling, waiting to take us home.

Tomorrow was another workday.

Under yet another new managing entity, my opportunities for advancement at work seemed to be waning, and answering to someone whose ideas differed so vastly from mine was becoming increasingly frustrating.

After sufficient rumination, consulting with those I knew who'd set up their own businesses, and many, many conversations with Pat, I made a critical decision to move on. I had been making independent decisions all my life—from peddling papers as a nine-year-old to getting my first real job at thirteen to joining the army and going to college—and those challenges were always exciting. Pat was endlessly supportive of anything I wanted to do. Being so independent herself, she understood the excitement in stepping out of the ordinary and trying new things (it also helped that she was still modeling and bringing in some extra cash if we ever needed it).

In my four years there, I had learned a great deal about producing films and large multimedia productions, as well as how live shows were created, written, developed, and staged. It was time for me to put that knowledge to work for myself. If others could do it, I could too.

CHAPTER 14

It was 1972, a presidential election year. President Nixon made an historic visit to China, U.S. ground troops were beginning to be withdrawn from Vietnam. The name Watergate hotel didn't mean much to anyone and was just a blurb buried deep in daily newspapers, gas was fifty-five cents a gallon, *The Godfather* movie was opening in theaters and Elton John's *Rocket Man* was moving up the Billboard charts. I was about to move up myself and open my own business as an independent producer. There were a million things to do.

Before leaving my previous job, I thought about getting a small business loan as a backstop in case it took longer than expected to land new clients. With my new business plan in hand, I happily walked into the Michigan National Bank in downtown Detroit, sat down with the loan officer, and was promptly turned down. That didn't deter me—my decision to move forward was already set.

I couldn't run a business out of my car, so I leased an office on the second floor of a small office building on the northwest side of Detroit. It was an ideal location along a main artery—James Couzens Highway—that could quickly get me anywhere in the city. Yes, that same James Couzens

I had drag raced on so frequently as a teenager.

My office window had a direct view of the alley (at least I knew that the garbage was being picked up each week), but there were benefits—it *did* come with free parking and an elevator.

I hoped to hire a secretary eventually, but for now, I simply purchased the essentials for a single office—one used desk, one chair, and a file cabinet. I'd gotten my business cards printed, my phone hooked up, and I was in business.

Why isn't the phone ringing yet? I wondered.

The afternoon of my first day in business, Pat came by with her parents and Heather to wish me luck. Seeing them standing there holding fresh flowers and a bottle of champagne, and hearing their positive comments, will forever be engrained in my mind. Pat's smile gave me confidence, but Heather—of course—took over, wanting to sit at my desk, check out the window, answer the phone, and run up and down the hall. It was wonderful to see others excited about my new endeavor, and I was brimming with confidence along with a touch of anxiety that accompanies the urge to get started.

"You're going to do great," my father-in-law said. He was always positive. Most of his life, being an independent painting contractor, he knew what it would take to successfully run a business of your own.

One thing I had learned as that young kid hanging around the newspaper garage (and later when getting my first the job at the drug store) was, like a firefly, I had to make myself visible. I immediately plunged into work, making what seemed like a thousand phone calls to try and set up meetings with potential clients.

To paraphrase what I once heard someone say—to be successful takes passion and a fire in your belly for what you want to accomplish, plus a refusal to be discouraged by a "no" once in a while.

As the newness and excitement of being an independent

producer subsided, questions raced through my mind. Had I made the right decision? Was there a way out if necessary? Where could I find a client who believed in me?

Do you know what the hell you're doing, kid? slipped in there as well.

"Yes, I do," I constantly told myself.

Before anything could be produced, I needed a client, and seeking out business was proving to be more difficult than I imagined. Large corporate clients were hesitant to work with individuals they didn't know, and they often preferred the security of a larger organization; building relationships with them would take months and months of consistent face time.

I spent as much time as possible out of my new office—it was depressing sitting there alone, staring out the window. Then one day, I received a phone call from a friend, John Long—I had worked with him at Jam Handy. He was now an account executive at a large advertising agency in Detroit. John was a straight talker who had no hidden agenda. I had stayed in contact with him and talked my way in to see him in his office from time to time, even though he was busy and might not have really wanted me there.

During our phone conversation, he told me his agency had been awarded a contract to produce a large motion picture for Chevrolet. Screen Gems from Hollywood was producing it and would be sending a crew out to film around the Detroit area. They needed a local producer to work with them: someone who knew the area, local resources, and could get things done.

"I thought of you," he said, adding, "Are you interested?"

Trying not to sound overeager, I responded, "Will the sun come up tomorrow? Absolutely, John. I am very interested and would love to do it. Tell me more. When do we start?"

"In two weeks. If you can come by my office tomorrow,

we'll go over the details."

I thanked him, hung up the phone, and let out a loud whoop of joy. *YES!* It was my first job as an independent producer. Over the next several weeks, I learned a great deal.

The film crew from Hollywood had a positive attitude, even when a car we were filming on the GM test track went out of control and slid into the 35-mm motion picture camera with wide angle lens, destroying that very expensive piece of equipment.

The scene called for the car to brake on a wet surface and come to a stop in a controlled manner. The water truck wet down the track and we rehearsed. It all went well. We wet it down again and the camera rolled. The car came at the camera, possibly a touch faster than during rehearsals, and at the given point, the driver hit the brakes. This time the car skidded awkwardly and didn't stop at the point it was supposed to. It almost took out the cameraman too. Luckily, an assistant had hold of his belt and pulled him away at the very last second.

By the next morning, the camera had been replaced and no filming time was lost. I was impressed. I'd been in situations at my last job where something like that could shut down production for days while someone sought approval to replace the camera.

At the end of each day's filming, the crew hung out in the hotel bar telling stories about films they'd worked on, including Hollywood stars they had encountered.

I was curious about what it was like working in Hollywood. "Just how competitive is it?" I asked the production manager.

He looked at me, with his forehead furrowed, and took another long drink of beer. "It's a very young town. Everyone seems to be in their 20s and would love to have your job. I'm holding onto mine," he said, sounding a bit proud. He was probably near fifty, and the lines on his face indicated he had weathered many production challenges.

The filming in Detroit took two weeks. It was edited in Hollywood, and when completed, I went to the screening. The film looked great.

Now with one client, I was back on the phone making calls trying to line up others. I had my eyes on *The Detroit News*. Two guys I'd worked with at Jam Handy were now running the paper's marketing department.

Ted Gropher, the vice president of marketing, was smart, a smooth talker, and always seemed to be a couple of steps ahead of the current conversation.

Dave Roche worked under Ted as the promotion manager. Together, they were responsible for marketing and promoting the paper, targeting well-established, sophisticated national ad agencies and large local advertisers. *The News*—with the largest daily circulation in the state—drew attention, but advertisers still needed to be reminded of the benefits.

Dave and I played on an adult ice hockey team two nights a week and often enjoyed post-game beers with other guys from the team. He was the ideal out-of-the-box thinker who wasn't afraid to take a gamble on a new idea. Maybe that's why we got along so well. I would stop in to see him whenever I was near the paper downtown, and one day while wrapping up a quick visit—probably talking hockey—Ted burst into Dave's office breathing heavily with an armful of artwork. It was near 5 p.m. and time to go home.

Ted looked at Dave. "I'm glad I caught you. I have to make a presentation to the publisher at 9 a.m. tomorrow and need all these graphics made into slides."

Slides were the usual presentation method, and producing a good slide was a process. The finished artwork had to be shot on film and taken to the color lab for processing. The lab in Detroit made its last daily processing run at 8 p.m., with the film ready for pickup around 10 p.m.

Then it had to be cut and mounted into slide mounts.

Dave knew the routine and what it took to prepare an effective presentation. Ted set the art down on Dave's desk. Taking a quick peek at the first couple of pieces of artwork, I could see Dave looked uneasy, and a bit surprised, asking Ted, "Can you move your meeting to later tomorrow or use something else? It's too late to get our photographer to shoot the art, get it to the lab, processed, mounted, and back first thing in the morning."

Ted wasn't budging and said with more urgency in his voice.

"I *really* need these. How can we do it?"

Dave was under pressure and really seemed stumped. I blurted out, "I can do it."

I couldn't believe I had just said that.

They both looked at me with a startled look.

Slightly frowning, Ted asked, "How do you plan to do that?"

"I know a cameraman who will shoot the art; I'll take it to his studio right now. After it's shot, I will personally deliver the film to the lab before their last run, pick it up as soon as it comes out, and go back his studio where we'll cut and mount the film. I can have it back to you by 8 in the morning."

Ted looked at Dave, then he turned to me and asked (with a touch of skepticism in his voice), "Are you sure you can get this done?"

"Yes. I won't let you down."

Dave seemed relieved and said, "I think that's the only way, Ted."

"OK," Ted responded.

I picked up the 35 pieces of art off Dave's desk. It contained the newspaper's highly confidential strategic future marketing plans.

"I can do it" were the most important words I could have said in that moment—I was lucky to have been in the right place at the right time. I delivered everything by 7:30 the next morning. Ted was pleased. It launched me down a path that held more business from the newspaper. I never said "no" to what they wanted done and always gave my honest opinion about it.

One major challenge they handed me involved the paper's annual sales and marketing presentation to major national advertisers and ad agencies. It was their most important event of the year, hosting hundreds of agency members in the main ballroom of the Plaza Hotel in New York and again the following week at the Hilton in downtown Chicago. Ted wanted something compelling to capture their attention and make a lasting impression.

Searching for the unusual, I recalled seeing a large inflatable poly-plastic room—about ten feet wide, twenty feet long, and eight feet high—in the JL Hudson department store downtown. It was set up in the middle of one of the store's departments and had rubber mats inside on the floor for children to go in to use as a play area. It was a clever way to keep kids busy while the parents shopped. There was always a great deal of activity surrounding it.

It piqued my interest so much so that I returned to the store and stood there for the longest time watching both parents and their children enjoy it. I wondered how I might use something like this to attract attention in a large ballroom filled with important advertising executives. Then, a light went on in my head: *reverse the action!* Rather than going inside it (because there would be too many people at our event for that), use as a powerful presentation piece in the center of the room with advertising executives standing on the outside, just as I was doing right then. Would it work with adults? Maybe.

I studied it further, and poking around the inflatable, saw a tiny label on the outside that held the manufacturer's phone number. Back in my office, I immediately called them and arranged a meeting at their facility in West Michigan.

It was out in the country away from any city. I was surprised upon arriving. The address was hand-painted on a piece of rusted aluminum that was hanging on an old fence surrounding what looked like a short, dirt runway partially covered with grass in the middle of a field. At one time, it might have been used for agricultural aircraft because on the far end of the overgrown runway sat an old hangar, just large enough for a single-engine crop duster.

I drove over to it, got out of the car, and walked in through the wobbly door of the Quonset-hut-like building and saw three older gentlemen in overalls playing cards at a small table lit by a single round light under a green shade. I must have gone back in time. It was like an old movie. Any moment, I expected to hear Claude Rains say to Humphrey Bogart, "I'm shocked, shocked to find gambling going on here," à la *Casablanca*.

When we talked on the phone, they sounded much more businesslike than they appeared here. Quickly putting that aside, we exchanged introductions. They had an inflatable already set up, like they'd said they would over the phone.

"Your inflatable is impressive. Can I see how it works?"

"Sure can," they said, as they slowly got up and moved toward it.

One gentleman stood near the blower that was running to keep it inflated. The other two stood next to me explaining technical details.

"It's twenty-eight feet long, ten feet wide, and eight feet high with flaps at each end. Holding it up are 4 ten-inch-round poly tubes filled with air that go up the sides and over the top. Everything is connected to the fan with this small tube running along the ground."

In between the tubes that held it up was plain poly material—kind of like projection screens, each "screen" about eight feet wide and six feet high—three on each side and one on either end. The inflatable was a bit larger than the one I had seen in the store, just as I hoped. I told them what I had in mind and noticed their eyebrows go up.

"That'll sure attract attention," one of them commented, chuckling.

I had them turn off the fan, and the structure slowly deflated.

"Now, can I see it fill up from totally deflated so I can time it?"

With my stopwatch in hand, they turned on the fan, and in 40 seconds, it was erect again. "Perfect!"

My plan was to leave it deflated sitting on a four-foot-high stage in the center of the ballroom while hundreds of ad agency members circulated around the room. On cue, it would inflate before their eyes. Once fully inflated, a multimedia visual presentation accompanied by music and narration would instantaneously run on all eight screens from sixteen slide projectors hidden inside the inflatable. The three-gentleman seemed interested, but I could tell they were still unconvinced. I continued, "We'll camouflage the projectors and build special covers so the heat and light from the bulbs won't burn the inflatable or wash out the visuals on the screens."

They passed a few glances back and forth at each other.

"Does inflation take the same amount of time every time?" I asked.

"It should," they quickly reassured me.

"OK then. Let's test it again to be sure." It did, and I told them to reserve the inflatable. "Same one, same size. Any questions?"

They didn't have any.

Back in the office I spent the next two weeks carefully writing my proposal and had a graphic designer prepare a rendering of what the entire room and event would look like.

My presentation to the paper, included Ted and Dave, plus VP of Sales. It went well. They had a few questions but I could tell looking around the conference table, they were enthralled. They were drawn to the idea of doing something different.

In the ballroom at the Plaza Hotel, the deflated poly room was lit from the outside by a series of rotating lights. The audience mingled around the room—digging into the many tables of shrimp and other finger foods—as rhythmic music played. The inflatable looked like a crumpled stack of plastic, merely serving as an interesting creative centerpiece. No one had any idea what it was, but everyone could see it no matter where they were in the room.

At the key moment, the house lights went down, and the room became completely dark. Flashing strobe lights took over as air slowly flowed into the tubes and the sculpture began moving in no set pattern. It simply appeared to be inflating to the pulsating beat of powerful drums and music.

The audience seemed frozen, captivated by what was happening. Then they began applauding. When it reached its full height, without pause, our soundtrack with narrative, dramatic high tempo music, and embedded cues triggering sixteen projectors began. The marketing presentation I had written and produced flashed across eight screens, encapsulating why *The Detroit News* was their most important advertising buy in Detroit. The message hit its mark. It was followed by live comments from the marketing VP.

It was a nail-biter for me and somewhat gutsy. There was no second chance. If it didn't work perfectly, the presentation would be a bust, and I would be out a client and a great deal of money. The striking event was a stunning success with tough New York ad buyers saying they had never seen anything quite like it before. It was the featured cover story on industry wide magazines.

That success led to more work from the paper, which included a major film centered on a revolutionary new printing plant they were building in suburban Detroit to replace the downtown plant. It was technologically advanced and would eventually be the paper's main facility. They wanted something dynamic, so I decided to produce the film documentary style. Nothing would be staged. For a while it felt like I was back in journalism, but this time, I hired a writer who I had previously worked with to draft the script. Bob Wicks had written scores of films and he did a terrific job outlining the message the paper wanted to convey. We would let the camera and the paper's employees tell the story.

Using a small film crew over a four-month period, a day or two each week, we carefully filmed and documented the dramatic key activities as the plant slowly came to life. It was a noisy film as the heavy construction equipment and work crews worked on while we filmed, and the giant, nearly two-story tall presses roared constantly as they were being put into use. In front of a background of ever-changing action, we captured the excitement as newspapers executives relayed the story of this advanced facility.

Mike, my very creative, yet at times, somewhat undisciplined cameraman, made me nervous from time to time by not sticking to what was in the script. I had reason to fire him a couple of times and asked myself, *Did I make a mistake by hiring him?* I ultimately stuck with my decision to keep him as he was talented, and it paid off. The film was a success and honored with awards, including one at the prestigious New York International Film and TV Festival.

My business was going well, as was Pat's modeling career. She had even gotten Heather a few jobs as a child model. At five years old, Heather just went along with it, and appeared on television once modeling children's clothes.

Pat modeled in Los Angeles a few times and always came home excited. She enjoyed working there. I was likewise thinking more about the West Coast now that my younger brother Les had moved out there to join my sister Irene and her husband. Pat and I talked about Los Angeles often. There were more opportunities out there for both of us—her modeling and acting career, and my business as well. The reality, however, was that my clients and contacts were in Detroit. Then, one day while scanning some industry publications, I saw that Fred Niles—a large Chicago production company—was looking for someone to run their Hollywood office. They also had offices in New York. In Chicago, Niles had a film studio, a recording studio, an animation department, and a staff of writers, directors, film editors, and producers numbering nearly fifty people, a little smaller, but similar to Jam Handy in Detroit. Niles produced major corporate stage productions, films, TV commercials, and some TV programs. Years later, his complex would be sold to Oprah Winfrey's Harpo Productions.

Not expecting anything to come of it, I decided to send them a resume. Two weeks later, Fred's assistant called and invited me to Chicago for an interview.

I met Fred in his modest office. He was pleasant, self-confident, had a smooth voice like you might hear on the radio somewhere, and seemed to me to also have a hefty ego.

He said the person running the Hollywood office wasn't doing the job. "I need someone out there who can turn it around." He studied my resume, asked copious questions, and listened to my ideas about how I could make that office successful again. I had a good feeling about the interview.

Fred thanked me for coming in and asked me to continue our discussion with his CFO, who was also in the meeting, to further go over my ideas. We left his office, and I was given a tour of the facility, meeting some of the people as we walked and talked. The CFO was a friendly, soft-spoken guy, who talked to me as if I already had the job. We spent the next hour, basically negotiating details and terms of a contract. Finally, he said, "I'll talk this over with Fred and we'll get back to you within a week."

I took a cab to the airport and flew home, not sure what their final decision would be, but I felt confident. Without a doubt, I was qualified for the job, having worked in television and with other production companies, plus running my own business. I knew not only how to write and produce but also what it took to develop new business.

A week later, I received a phone call from Fred. It was brief. "We'd love to have you join our company," he said. We briefly reviewed the final terms I had negotiated with the CFO and a contract arrived a couple of days later which I signed. It was a major life-changing decision.

CHAPTER 15

J ust a few months before the Niles opportunity sprung up, I had told my sister Irene, "When the right job comes along, Pat and I would seriously consider leaving Detroit for LA." She and Paul, her husband, were excited about the prospect of us possibly moving to the coast, and wished me luck.

A month later, we received a distressing call from Irene. Paul had suffered a heart attack and died suddenly while they were in Las Vegas for the weekend. I immediately flew out to LA to be with her. She was in shock and talked about possibly moving back to Detroit. Les, who was living in LA, was as surprised to hear that as we were. Pat and I were saddened by Paul's sudden, tragic death, and personally it put a temporary damper on my enthusiasm about looking to move west.

Now, however, with a signed contract, moving to California was becoming a reality. The seed had been planted years earlier when my three friends and I had driven to Hollywood on that post-graduation trip after high school. I had visualized it at the time and remember thinking: *It would be nice to live out here.* That seed obviously took hold, sprouted, and here we were.

We aggressively plunged into selling our house and finding a new place to live in Los Angeles—Niles Productions was paying all the moving costs.

The easy part was selling our house as we lived in an excellent area north of Detroit. The house was in top-notch condition, priced to sell, and it didn't take long before a bidding war ensued, meaning we didn't need to reduce our asking price. It sold quickly.

While the sale went smoothly, shipping our belongings was a hassle. American Van Lines was moving everything, including our classic Porsche. I was already in LA looking for an apartment while Pat was taking care of the details at home, and she was not comfortable with the people packing and loading our things when she called me, sounding uneasy.

"These guys don't seem to care about how they're packing. One of them keeps commenting about how much he would love to have the two antique Spanish swords mounted over the fireplace—I told him they're not for sale. They are making me nervous, eyeing all our belongings."

"Don't worry," I reassured her, "everything will be fine. They move people all the time; they know what they're doing."

After the furniture truck was loaded and was on its way, Pat and Heather stayed with her parents for the next two weeks so as not to arrive too much ahead of our furniture. I had a couple of apartments to show them when they got to L.A., and we quickly settled on one. We moved in, and for a few days, slept on two mattresses we'd purchased to put on the floor until our furniture arrived.

I thought, *Nothing has changed*, and recalled doing something similar when we moved to our first apartment in Grand Rapids nearly ten years prior, smiling fondly at the memory of camping out in our empty apartment, eating TV dinners.

Up until that point, everything had gone without a hitch,

but the promised delivery date for our furniture had come and gone—the truck hadn't arrived. We began to worry and called the movers. The driver apparently decided to stop in Oklahoma and visit his girlfriend on the way to LA. Someone messed up big-time, though we were never sure what really happened in Oklahoma. When the truck did arrive in LA, it had a different driver than the one in Detroit. The crew, oblivious to the problems we'd encountered, simply unloaded the furniture in our apartment.

Our two Spanish swords were missing—maybe the original driver dropped them off in Oklahoma. Because they were not specifically listed on the bill of lading, the moving company hesitated to reimburse us, but after applying some pressure, showing them photos, and threatening legal action, they agreed to pay a small amount, although nothing near the swords' actual value.

Then we got another surprise: our Porsche was damaged. When loading the truck, someone had apparently stuck some objects next to the car, which then slid into it and put a crease in the car's door from top to bottom. The moving company paid for the damage, but looking back, I wish we also would have checked the mileage—perhaps the driver unloaded it in Oklahoma as well so he could take his girlfriend for a spin. Regardless, now with furniture, we finally felt settled in our new apartment.

On TV, in August of 1974, we watched Richard Nixon resign as President and Vice President Ford being sworn in as President of the United States. It was riveting and called to mind my interviews with President Ford years earlier when he was the house minority leader in Congress.

Pat was busy registering Heather at a nearby school. At six years old, she was our princess, a bundle of energy, smiles, love, and excitement. Although most of her day was spent around Heather, Pat still found time to make her vital calls and visits to film studios so she could introduce herself to talent agents and casting directors. In Hollywood, whether modeling or acting, talent is hired through agents who are in close contact with the studios' casting directors.

Meanwhile, Irene was talking less about moving back to Detroit. We were relieved; it was reassuring to have family in town but more so to know my sister was starting to settle back into a little normalcy after such a traumatic and tragic loss.

I called the woman who previously ran the Niles office in Hollywood and was surprised to learn that she had been working out of her apartment for the past couple of months prior to losing her job. I was eager to meet her and pick up the files, expecting an abundance of client contact information. Disappointingly, all she handed me was a small, shallow cardboard box with some disorganized old letters and papers; she had little regarding clients or associates she was in contact with while running the office. I couldn't help but notice the similarity between her and that disheveled box of documents and just could not figure out how she had got the job. I asked her if anyone from Chicago had ever been out to check on the office.

"Right after I was hired—several months ago—one of the execs came by, but I haven't seen anyone since. A few months later, they cancelled the lease, and I was told to work out of my apartment until we found a new office. That never happened, and they let me go."

"I'm sorry about that," I said and picked up the small box of miscellaneous papers, none of which contained anything of substance.

As I moved toward the door to step out into the hall, she remarked, "Good luck. I sent the rest of the files back to Chicago." (I had talked with them previously, and they hadn't received any files.)

"If you need anything else, just give me a call." The slight smirk on her face divulged her true meaning, though. "Tough luck. I'm not giving you anything else."

I thought to myself, *Call you? Sure, right!*

It then struck me: I signed a contract to run an office and was expecting a trove of client files to get me started. Nothing existed. The perception of a Niles production office on the West Coast didn't correspond with reality at that moment, and what was presented to me when accepting the job didn't align with the facts before me now. What had I gotten myself into? I was too busy to think about it for long and was determined to make it work out.

Well, I had always wanted to live on the West Coast, and here I was with a well-paying job that was guaranteed for at least two years. I was basically building the business in Los Angeles from scratch—*déjà vu*. I did that for my own business in Detroit, and now was doing it for someone else.

I found and sublet an office from a guy who owned a small PR firm, just him and his secretary. Part of the deal was she would answer the phone and type correspondence as needed. The office was in a perfect location in a high-rise in Westwood near the UCLA campus, close to the I-405 freeway. In LA, everything is spread out, so daily freeway travel is a given and being close to one is a must to get anywhere quickly (well, maybe not *quickly*; any freeway before ten in the morning or after three in the afternoon was guaranteed to be gridlocked).

Subletting the office was short-lived. The secretary didn't hold regular hours, and the few times she did type something for me, it was sloppy with errors. When answering the phone, she sounded more impatient than friendly, and that doesn't work when clients call. I thought, *this is a sorry situation.* I decided to move to our own office in the same building and hire my own secretary.

I focused my efforts on corporate clients such as Toyota, Suzuki Motorcycles, Carnation, and other major companies on the West Coast. In LA and Hollywood, "producers" are ubiquitous, and most of them hope to make it to the large Hollywood film factories; they weren't very much interested in producing shows and films for corporate clients.

Consistently working the phones every day—all day— to set up face-to-face meetings was the only way any business would be coming our way. I tried to be as visible as possible with potential clients and did my research before calling them. How do they communicate with their nationwide network of dealers and distributors? How can I help them with that?

Still buried deep in my subconscious were the words, "They don't want you there." I sometimes had that feeling when approaching a new client and had to remind myself that if they didn't want me there, why did they agree to meet? In that same vein, if someone I was calling appeared to be a negative person, I quickly moved on.

A few years prior, I had met the vice president of sales and marketing at Suzuki Motorcycles when he was working in Detroit for a different company. It was a casual meeting, but we seemed to connect, so naturally he was one of my first calls when I heard he was now working in LA for Suzuki.

Gene was a tall, friendly guy who always greeted you with a big smile and a warm handshake. He had a very positive attitude, as sales people usually have. He was responsible for marketing Suzuki motorcycles.

I didn't know much about motorcycles and wasn't familiar with words like *fairings*, *saddles*, *cruisers*, *touring*, *off road*, and the other cycling jargon. The only time I had ever been on a motorcycle was when my brother Les had taken me for a ride on his. I was very uncomfortable zipping around with nothing between me and the pavement. Regardless, I was happy to make contact with Gene again.

Suzuki was introducing a couple of new bikes, and Gene gave me the opportunity to produce a short film about each of them. Those films turned out well and would be used as part of the annual national dealer meeting Suzuki would be holding in Washington DC, where it was launching a new rotary-powered motorcycle as well.

"I need to introduce the Rotary bike in a dramatic fashion—our dealers will be coming in from across the country to see it," he said.

I didn't hesitate: "I would love to produce the entire meeting for you, Gene, and can make the entire introduction compelling and unique."

My idea was to introduce the motorcycle sitting on a nearly invisible, radio-controlled platform built specifically for the reveal. It had to be strong enough and large enough to support the weight of the motorcycle as it came on stage through a long, darkened tunnel filled with fog, dramatic lighting, and a pulsating rumble of dynamic sounds. Gene was a natural salesman and loved big and dramatic ideas. He liked this one as did his bosses. We were awarded the contract to write and produce the show.

The planned launch almost turned into a disaster. The black platform, containing the remote-control device was large, seven feet long, three feet wide and eighteen inches high. It was shipped from our Chicago office and they failed to take into consideration that we were setting the stage and rehearsing on Labor Day weekend. When the shipment was not at the hotel on Saturday morning as it needed to be for set up and rehearsals, I called the freight office in Washington. The dispatch person told me, "It's a holiday and there is nothing on the bill of lading saying to deliver the shipment this weekend. Sorry it's too late to schedule it for today. Tuesday is the earliest we can get it to you." I told him that that wouldn't work as Tuesday morning was the day of our show. I pleaded with him—it must have been for the better part of forty-five minutes, exploring any way we could make this happen. We weren't making any progress. He said "I'm sorry," so many times that his words became hollow. Out of desperation, I switched my approach and asked, "Can we pick it up ourselves?"

"I don't know if that is possible," he said. Trying to contain my frustration and growing anger over the situation, I asked, "Can you please find out?'

"Hold on," he said, sounding a bit annoyed himself by this time. And the phone went silent. I waited and then another person came on the phone. I repeated my story, yet again. Finally, he said what I wanted to hear. "Yes, you can pick it up yourselves."

Why didn't the dispatch person simply say that? I bit my tongue, thanked him, and said we would be there within the next two hours. My stage manager was beginning the show setup for rehearsals in the hotel ballroom. I pulled him out and we scrambled to rent a van and went to the airport freight office.

The day of the show, with several hundred dealers and Suzuki executives in the audience, we were ready. Finally, as the highlight of the hour-long meeting arrived, the words, "Something new is coming!" boomed over the huge sound system hung from the ceiling, the room suddenly went dark, and the music and magic began. The audience gazed in wonderment as the motorcycle came on stage through the black tunnel seemingly floating on air on the black platform in gleaming light to the dealer's applause. Gene, smiling from ear to ear, stepped forward to enthusiastically detail the bike's strong selling points. He seemed relieved and the dealers were enthused. The launch went perfectly and I felt good about what we had done for them. I let our Chicago office know of their screwup.

I would now be moving on to a new client, beer.

Olympia brewing company near Seattle contacted me about a large event they had in mind for hundreds of their beer distributors. Would I like to talk with them about it?

"Yes, of course," I said, and flew to Seattle and drove south to the small town of Tumwater—where the brewery was located—near Olympia, the state capital.

The brewery was built in 1896 by a German immigrant

and he began selling Olympia beer in 1902. Olympia would be celebrating its 75th anniversary.

The brewery was nestled among the towering trees of the great Northwest. Arriving, there was no mistake I was near a brewery as the air was thick with the aroma of hops and ingredients found in beer. Walking into the lobby, I noticed a tasting room off to the side with a line of people waiting for a free sample. It reminded me of what we did on hot summer days as kids in Detroit. We went to the Vernors plant near downtown on Woodward Avenue and stood in line for a free Vernors.

I was given a tour of the brewery by the VP of sales, and in the cafeteria, I was surprised to find beer available for employees. That was something I had never seen before in a company's cafeteria.

Over the next few weeks, I traveled to Tumwater several times and Chicago was getting nervous about the costs. I urged them to be patient and had a good feeling we would be awarded the contract to write and produce the entire show that was going to be held in LA. I was right.

We created a live one-hour stage production, complete with cast members singing praises of Olympia Beer's history and highlighting the future success distributors could expect.

Al, my stage manager—from our Chicago office—was a real challenge, and difficult to work with. Following one of the rehearsals, I found him backstage drinking. He became argumentative when I told him there's no drinking allowed while working.

"It's a beer client; I'm just supporting their product," he mumbled.

"No," I said. "We support the client by staging a good show, not by drinking on the job." Unfortunately, the client overheard our confrontation. I feared if there were any mistakes in the show, the client would blame it on crew members drinking. The ramifications could be many. The show came off without a hitch, and I told our Chicago office that I would never be using Al again.

We produced many TV commercials in Chicago but not LA. I didn't know much about producing TV commercials other than the fact that they were outrageously expensive to produce. A friend of mine worked with Carnation—headquartered in Los Angeles—and was the product manager handling their cat foods. I introduced him to one of our Chicago account executives who presented a unique concept in TV co-op advertising to him. He immediately liked it and we were awarded the contract to produce a large package of TV commercials for his products out of our LA office.

That wet Fred's beak. He wanted us to increase our production of commercials in LA, but we didn't have a studio full of equipment like in Chicago, and he wasn't about to invest in any. His idea was to partner with someone who already had everything in Hollywood.

A very wealthy friend of his in Chicago told him, Dwight Chapin, former President Nixon confidant, was an executive at a Hollywood production company and might be a good partner. Fred called me and asked me to arrange to meet with Chapin.

"Find out what his company is all about," said Fred. "Explore if they might be interested in partnering with us."

I called Chapin and arranged to meet with him in his office near Hollywood and Vine. He was friendly and very tidy, dressed in a dark, tailored suit with pant creases as sharp as a razor. Not a hair on his head was out of place and his fingers looked recently manicured. He was almost too perfect. We talked—or, I should say, *he* talked—and he seemed to me to be rather pompous, with a large ego, and couldn't stop telling me how important he and his company were. I had a different impression and told Fred that Chapin's company was similar to others in Hollywood with one difference, they provided the theater Merv Griffin used for his popular TV show. Fred wanted to meet him anyway, and for the first time since I began running the Niles west coast office, nearly two years earlier, he came out to Los Angeles. Fred and I met with Chapin, in the theater. That seemed like a strange place to discuss business. He wasn't any more impressed than I was with him or what he had to offer, and finally decided to give up the partnership idea. Maybe there was a clash of egos.

In Hollywood, ideas, some good and some not so much so, seem to flow like water and a production company called me to see if we might want to partner with them and create short films of rock groups to distribute to TV stations—something that a few groups were doing but had not been widely done yet. I was enthused but Chicago wasn't, as it involved laying out money on a new venture with no guaranteed return. They didn't grasp the possibilities, and told me to decline. It was really too bad, with music videos being such a cutting-edge idea at the time, and a couple of years later becoming the backbone of launching new TV channels like MTV.

There was much going on in the country. It was the Bicentennial year; Jimmy Carter, a peanut farmer from Georgia, was about to move into the White House. There was an outbreak of a new deadly disease called Legionnaires', the Space Shuttle Enterprise was being rolled out, inflation was on the rise, and two guys named Jobs and Wozniak started a revolution by introducing the Apple 1 and Apple II personal computers.

Pat was making inroads with her career, getting new roles in TV and films, though it took many auditions and considerable leg work to get them.

She often said, "Going to auditions in New York was somewhat easier than in Hollywood. My agent in New York sent me out to auditions when they knew I was right for a part. Here, in Hollywood, my agent sends me out on everything, whether I'm right for the part or not, and there's often a long line of beautiful girls auditioning. It feels like they don't know what they are looking for, and they even admit sometimes, that they don't."

One time she met, just by chance, a very well-known and high-powered Hollywood director on one of the studios lots.

"He was very friendly and we began talking. I was impressed that he wanted to know more about me and my career. I was thinking how lucky I was to meet him and he seemed genuinely interested, but I didn't expect what he did next." she told me.

He followed her home, knocked on the apartment door and expected she would invite him in. She didn't. She never got any parts in his films after that encounter.

It's Hollywood after all, and things happen in a town brimming with beautiful, young, aspiring actresses looking for their big break and others looking to give it to them—for a price.

As the calendar turned over to 1977, our office was getting busier. I decided help was needed and hired Danny, a young, positive, enthusiastic guy in his early twenties. He always had a smile on his face, talked a lot, interrupted often, and was full of fresh ideas and questions, those same questions I had frequently asked myself: "Do we *have to* do it this way? Is there a better way?"

I gave him a list of potential new clients with instructions to use his energies to contact them and set up meetings for us. Danny was new in the business and I wanted to go with him to make sure we were making a good impression.

I recalled that production manager a few years earlier telling me that "people in Hollywood in their early twenties want your job," but I never felt insecure about that with Danny. If he wanted my job, he could earn it. I knew who I was.

Two years flew by, and my contract was coming up for

renewal. I had probably accomplished more and brought in more business in LA for our company than they'd ever had before. They offered me a bounce in salary and an extension of my contract, but I was unsure.

Despite all the unknowns at that time, I was looking to the future. Our family would be growing with a second child, Donovan, and I had exciting ideas and dreams to chase.

My itch to do more creative things on my own had come back. I wanted to branch out, set my own agenda, and build my own identity again, so I garnered up my courage and made the difficult decision to say "goodbye" to working for someone else. I was about to embark on another new adventure.

CHAPTER 16

L eaving that secure job and summoning up the courage to seek my own dreams felt like reaching out for fireflies once again—their mysterious glimmering lights beckoned me to extend my reach until one flew through my fingers.

I have always been independent, charting my own course, and it took me over thirty years to accept and openly acknowledge that.

Especially growing up, I had been banging heads and wits with people I thought were trying to prevent me from succeeding. I strived for independence in a very crowded house, and if I wanted to succeed—to truly get anywhere— I wasn't going to get any positive direction there. I was going to have to do it on my own.

The home on Mark Twain Street where I grew up in Detroit was a safe sanctuary for a large family that, from time to time, was filled with laughter and merriment. It was also an explosive place that blasted out negativity and verbal abuse.

My ideas were often dismissed or ridiculed with discouraging remarks from family members whom I loved and needed the most. I quickly developed deep-seated feelings of mistrust and wariness, often shielding my dreams and ideas for fear they would either be laughed at, crushed, or stolen.

Maybe my father's anger stemmed from a realization that his hopes and dreams were slowly fading away under the weight of supporting such a large family; I just happened to be one of those weights.

I also have come to realize that the discouraging, knife-like comments often received from my older siblings whenever I tried to learn something on my own—"You're not going to learn anything reading those books," or "When are you going to learn how to play that thing?" while I practiced guitar at the age of eleven—were their defense mechanisms. My creativity and independence didn't fit with their thinking, so they put me down, maybe to cover their own inadequacies and mediocrity.

I have come a long way in overcoming the damage caused by an unsupportive family environment when I wanted to try something never done before or take a different path. Now, I finally understand their actions. It wasn't me; it was they who had to deal with their own lack of accomplishment and short-sightedness.

Upon pausing to reflect, I have asked myself, *What if I hadn't heeded my father's sarcastic comment, "Don't work in a god damn factory"?* Was that his way of saying he wanted the best for me or just another in a stream of negative comments that flowed from his mouth like a faucet? Ironically, his sarcasm helped me make a life-changing decision to enlist in the Army.

Was that store owner's question to me, "Why don't you go to college?" a sign he really cared or just casual conversation? Regardless, I decided to take the challenge and answer that question.

And Pat's invitation in college, "Come on over, I'll introduce you to the people in the media department," touched me deeply, as she seemed to really care. That invitation and my decision to accept it turned out to be life-changing.

Though made at a relatively young age, these were decisions that I will forever carry in my pocket because, in many ways, they were the moments that set my life's course. A few fears and doubts still lurk like deep wounds that heal slowly, but wounds, similar to scratches on a car, often can be removed over time with consistent rubbing and buffing. Though they are indeed disappearing, at certain angles, in a certain light, there's still a faint indication of what was once there. They might never go away completely, so I choose to move forward without dwelling on them.

I will succeed despite what I faced early on; I have continually told myself. That bold determination is what has pushed me forward on my own, again and again, to reach out for something better. Success isn't easy, but if it were, anyone could have it.

I paid my dues and never could have forged my own future without making gutsy decisions that proved to be mostly correct (and sometimes... not so much).

Some decisions resulted in work that touched thousands of lives, some decisions led to being sought out for advice by the heads of major corporations, and other decisions called for the courage and intelligence to interview future presidents and lawmakers.

If it were not for the challenges I faced growing up that pushed me to break free from my negative self-talk and think independently, I may have simply followed the crowd toward groupthink and conformity. Surprisingly, I was able to turn that turmoil around to make myself stronger and take control on my terms.

I have volunteered my time, energy, and ideas toward working with young people in a positive way, encouraging them to set and reach their goals. I understand the kid who is fighting to be heard and recognized—I was that kid too.

Now, with my own wonderful family, I encourage hold,

creative ideas, and positive thinking, no matter how strange something may sound. Exploring the new and different is not only exciting but also the only way to grow. Let your imagination flow freely and great things will happen. There have been many critical decisions whose consequences helped shape me, and there will be many more to further chisel away and smooth the remaining rough edges.

Stepping out on my own made me as excited, happy, and satisfied as that kid walking home after a full day playing ice hockey on the frozen Detroit pond in temperatures nearing the single digits: I couldn't wait until the sun came up to do it all over again the next day.

I still look forward to tomorrow's sunrise and still notice the fireflies light up the evening sky. Making hard decisions will continue to extend my grasp and shape me in the future, but some decisions aren't difficult. Every day I look at Pat's smile, kiss her, and say, "I love you."

That's an easy decision.

CONNECT WITH THE AUTHOR

Follow Ed Tar Memoir on Facebook

LinkedIn: http://www.linkedin.com/in/ed-tar-b4407b4a

Instagram: http://www.instagram.com/edtarassociates

Website: www.edtarauthor.com

Email: etieta@aol.com